Gerrit Smith

Speeches and Letters of Gerrit Smith

On the Rebellion

Gerrit Smith

Speeches and Letters of Gerrit Smith
On the Rebellion

ISBN/EAN: 9783337018054

Printed in Europe, USA, Canada, Australia, Japan

Cover: Foto ©ninafisch / pixelio.de

More available books at **www.hansebooks.com**

SPEECHES AND LETTERS

OF

GERRIT SMITH

(FROM JANUARY, 1863, TO JANUARY, 1864)

ON THE

REBELLION.

New-York:

JOHN A. GRAY & GREEN, PRINTERS, STEREOTYPERS, AND BINDERS,

FIRE-PROOF BUILDINGS,

CORNER OF FRANKFORT AND JACOB STREETS.

1864.

LETTER TO GOVERNOR SEYMOUR.

PETERBORO, January 12th, 1863.

HON. HORATIO SEYMOUR:

DEAR SIR: I have read your Message. Although I belong to no party, I belong to a country. Although there are no party interests for me to promote and adjust myself to, I feel the preciousness of the interests of my country, and am deeply and abidingly concerned for their safety. Seldom more than when reading the Message have I felt the great peril of those interests. For I remember that the utterer of its dangerous doctrines is emphatically, if not indeed preëminently, the mouthpiece of a party comprising nearly half the voters of the Free States. I remember too what great weight with his party have the words of a gentleman of commanding talents, high culture, multiplied influential public relations, bland and winning manners, admired social and domestic life. How could I fail to fear that the Democratic Party, if not already fully identified with these dangerous doctrines, will by force of such commendations of them soon become so?

1st. I find denunciation in the Message, but no denunciation of the rebels. The Cotton States and the New-England States do in your esteem share about equally in the guilt of the Rebellion. New-England, because she suffered her Garrison to write against Slavery, and her Phillips to talk against it, is in your eyes as criminal as the bloody men who flew at the throat of their unoffending country. New-England who, to help put them down, promptly armed hundreds of thousands of her cherished sons and promptly poured out scores of millions of her wealth, has no less of your censure and no more of your favor than have those bloody men. And yet you propose to put down the Rebellion! But how can this be done if nearly half of us are like yourself? How could we have the heart to do it even at little cost—much less at the required cost—if the rebels are no worse than the people of New-England? And how, if we *had* the heart, would it be practicable, should you succeed, as is your too manifest intent, in arraying the Western and Central States against New-England instead of Rebeldom?

2d. I see you still regret that the Satanic compromise proposed two years ago was not adopted. I call it Satanic because it was

4

GERRIT SMITH ON THE REBELLION.

to be a compromise between two guilty parties at the sole expense—and this too an overwhelming expense—of an innocent third party. Fresh outrages were to be heaped upon the negroes—ay and eternized. The malignity of this Democratic compromise, which not a few Republicans also favored, (for there are Republicans too who are capable of being satanized,) is equaled only by its meanness. That they, who could propose further and greater crimes against the guiltless and helpless, could still make much account of their Bibles and Churches, argues either their matchless delusion or their matchless brazenness. I do not say they would have made themselves better by burning up their Bibles and Churches: but I do say that they would have thereby made themselves infinitely more consistent.

3d. "The claim of power under martial law" you indignantly and utterly refuse to admit. You say that this claim "asserts that the President may in his discretion declare war." I do not believe that it does, and I never before heard that it does. You say that it "exalts the military power of the President above his Constitutional rights." I reply that this power is specifically one of those rights, inasmuch as the Constitution makes him the Head of the Army. I admit that he has no other official rights than what the Constitution gives him; and you should admit that it is only from martial law, or, in other words, the law of civilized warfare, that he can learn the measure of his rights as Head of the Army. You say that this "measure is fixed by the Constitution." Rather is it fixed by this martial law which you disparage. It also changes with this law, which changes with the progress of civilization. It is true that Congress has power to prescribe rules for war. But, on the other hand, it is not only true that it could not provide for a large share of the cases in which the Head of the Army might find himself; but also true that this power of Congress is to be exercised within the limits and according to the character of martial law. So long as that law shall forbid the poisoning of food or water, or the killing of prisoners, or the selling of them into slavery, Congress has no power to authorize these barbarisms. That a nation may carry on war according to its own laws, be they what they will, Christendom would never suffer. These laws must be conformed to the law of civilized warfare. If it is true, as recently reported, that the rebels shot twenty prisoners because they were black, and if also their government shall approve it, then will this enormous violation of the conventions of war not only go far to reveal the character of the rebels to the eyes of Europe ; but it will also go far to damage their cause with her.

4th. Scouting as you do the doctrine of martial law, it is not strange that you deny the right of the Head of the Army to lay hands, even in time of war, on persons in a loyal State. Indeed, you do not admit that he may on persons in a revolted one. You decline saying whether such a State has lost any of its rights. Your language clearly implies that it has not lost them all. Here, as elsewhere in the Message, you treat the rebels as more "sinned against than sinning." Doubtless you hold that State sovereignty can never die:—no, not even in a State whose people have all turned traitors. Possibly, however, you would admit that the Head of the Army has the right to dispose of the hundred Missouri traitors, who just within the north line of Arkansas are plotting and promoting the destruction of our army and country. But how farcical the distinction that he may not dispose of them if, availing themselves of your theory, they return a mile, and claim that they can now perpetrate their treason with impunity, because they are again in their loyal State of Missouri! Moreover, Missouri might, at the time, be the principal seat of the war, and the very State in which traitors could most peril and damage our cause. Whilst writing this letter, I learn that Springfield in Missouri is besieged by rebels. Does not our army there need the right to make the quick and sure military dispositions of both open and suspected traitors? Surely it does: and what folly, not to say what treason, to deny the right, simply because Springfield is in one of the really or nominally loyal States! Upon your theory a single State, and though no larger than Rhode Island or Delaware, might, under its mask of loyalty, by harboring traitors and protecting their operations, accomplish the betrayal of the country into the hands of the enemy. Surely, surely, our nation could not have meant to leave herself at such fatal disadvantage. She could not have failed to mean that, in time of war, her military power should be free everywhere within her borders to deal with traitors in its own sure and summary ways where they could not safely be intrusted to slow, uncertain, and what, even though in a professedly loyal State, might prove to be *disloyal* civil proceedings. If it be but one State that has broken out in war against the nation, the war power nevertheless is entitled to its paramount rule in every State so long as the war shall continue. So long it must have the right to practice in every State its own means for saving all the States. The military power may not dispose of a man in a loyal State! Amazing error! It may not only arrest him, but reduce his dwelling to ashes. The Head of the Army may, and should, order the arrest of the people of Chambersburgh, ay and the burning of their town, if he is convinced that it is, and if unburnt will remain, a nest of traitors. Had it been your purpose so to cripple the President and his army, as to render the country an easy prey to its enemy, you could not have written more effectually to this end than you have done. You say: "The unlimited, uncontrolled despotic power claimed under martial law is of itself a reason why it can not be admitted." The answer is, that for this very reason the power must be admitted. No nation ever did or ever can stand, that does not make martial law supreme in time of war. The main reason why the comparatively petty South is still able to resist the gigantic North, is that the one has and the other has not a Democratic Party to hold it back from an unrestricted and successful prosecution of the war. The

rebels "let slip *their* dogs of war." But the Democrats are constantly intent on leashing *ours*. You will argue the danger of the
abuse of this martial law. But that will be no argument against
the necessity of the law. It will be an argument only against the
madness of running rashly into war.

5th. You deny the right of the Head of the Army to proclaim
liberty to the slaves of loyalists. You seem to believe that our
government must not only not *intend* injuries to loyalists, but
must so conduct the war that not even *incidental* injuries, though
afterward paid for, shall ever befall them. The military commander is however at as full liberty to burn the dwelling of the
loyalist as of the rebel, if in his judgment the necessities of war
call for it. It is his right to weaken the foe by calling away from
him white or red or black men. He may strengthen his ranks by
inviting to them the minor sons of loyal fathers and the apprentices of loyal masters. But if he may invite these to break away
from their just and natural relations, how much more may he invite slaves, be it those of rebels or loyalists, to break away from
their infinitely unjust and unnatural relations! He may not think
the slaves to be in any wise fit for his ranks. He may (and this
would be an entirely justifying reason) invite them to leave their
rebellious or loyal masters simply because he would thereby reduce the force which produces the food and other elements of
Southern subsistence and Southern success. In all this the commander would not be saying that the relation of master and slave
is any less moral than the other relations referred to. He would
but be saying that he feels bound to do whatever he can in accordance with the laws and usages of civilized warfare to weaken
his foe and strengthen himself.

6th. Our work, as you interpret it, is to save the Constitution
as it was and to "restore our Union as it was before the outbreak
of the war." Right here, at this great error, is it probable that our
nation will perish, if perish it must. The breaking out of the
Rebellion found the nation so debauched by slavery as to be incapable of meeting the Rebellion on the one square and simple
issue of putting it down. For thirty or forty years it had cherished, not to say worshiped, slavery : and nearly all its contests
during that time for the Constitution and the Union were virtually
contests for slavery. Hence she had scarcely come to blows with
the South before the North found her people divided by feigned,
false, impertinent and ruinous issues. Loud and incessant was the
cry, that the Constitution and Union must be restored. The
Democrats and pro-slavery Republicans meant a restoration to
the intensely pro-slavery interpretation that the one and to the intensely pro-slavery character that the other had reached when the
Rebellion broke out. The anti-slavery Republicans were for restoring the Constitution and Union to what they were held to be
in those early days of the Republic, when slavery was looked upon
as sectional and liberty national. A part of the abolitionists said
that the Constitution is anti-slavery, and that therefore in the

name of the Constitution, as well as in the name of God, the Union should also be anti-slavery. And another part said that the Constitution is pro-slavery, and that they preferred no Union at all to a Union under a pro-slavery Constitution.

Oh! had we but been uncorrupted by slavery, how quickly would we have put down the Rebellion, if indeed there could in that case, have been a Rebellion to put down! We should then have wasted no time, and produced no division amongst ourselves, by talking about the Union, the Constitution, or even the Country. Our one purpose then would have been to put down the rebels—and to put them down irrespectively of the bearing it might have on whatever interests. Naked plunderers and murderers were these entirely unwronged rebels: and they should have been put down with as total a disregard of consequences, as would characterize the single purpose of a stern father in putting down his revolted child. Who doubts that with such a disregard they had been put down instantly? Suppose that scoundrels in Utica—your adopted and my native home—had, with arms in their hands, and using them too, seized her funds, her fire-engines, and her other corporate property, and that you had, at the time, been her Mayor; would you have sent to the Common Council a Message of the tone and character of that you have just sent to the Legislature? Would you have sought in it to divide her citizens upon a multiplicity of issues respecting the future condition of her Fire Department, her funds and other interests? Oh no! oh no!! You could have made no Democratic and no other gain by such an insane policy. You would, beyond a doubt, have sought to unite them in the one purpose and one endeavor to subdue and punish the miscreants; ay, to subdue and punish them, come what might of Fire Department, Funds, or even Utica herself. I am wrong—they would already have been thus united. Such union would have been the necessary result of the outrage. Only bad counsels and partisan influences could have disunited them. The people of the North were united when they heard of the bombarding of Sumter. But alas our good and patriotic President temporized! The spirit, which should have been taken at the flood, was allowed time to subside. Hundreds of thousands of lives, and directly and indirectly thousands of millions of dollars have already been the penalty of this mistake: and only too reasonable is the fear that the loss of the nation will be needed to complete the penalty. How surely and how quickly would he at that time but for the timidity and hesitancy, which grew out of his pro-slavery education, have saved our wealth and toil from this oppressive taxation, our tens of thousands of bereaved families from their sorrows, and our country from the appalling prospect of her ruin! The Rebellion should have been shot dead at once. Whoever denies it proves therein that he is insensible of its infernal character, and knows not how to deal with such a crime. Or rather, whoever denies it makes room thereby for the suspicion that he sympathizes with the Rebellion and is a participant in the crime.

At once should the President have brought out the Big Emancipation Gun: and he should have so charged it, and so aimed it, as
not to spare one shred of slavery in all the land. The Rebellion
would have been ended by the first fire. And what right had the
rebels to our shrinking and delay ?—rebels who, without the least
provocation, so malignantly and murderously struck at our all ?—
at the life of our country, and therefore at our all ?

7th. What a sad exhibition of the power of ambition and party
over a great intellect, combined with a gentle and refined spirit, is
your insisting that slavery shall be reëstablished ; that the Southern "elements of production *must* be unimpaired ;" and, that
nothing short of this "*can* command the support of the majority of
the American people "! Yes, even now, when, if there ever was,
there is no longer any Constitutional obstacle in the way of the
slave's freedom ; even now when the slaveholder has himself open-
ed the prison-door—you are still determined that he shall remain
in bondage, and his children and children's children after him—still
determined that this shall continue to be a land in which multiplying millions have no right to husband nor wife nor children nor wages
nor Bibles nor schools nor to aught else but stripes and insults, tortures of the body and tortures of the soul. You are indeed to be
pitied. You were not made to be what you are. You were made
to be a strong, and helpful, and sustaining brother among your
poor, and needy, and weak brethren : not an object of terror but a
tower of safety to them. You were made not to bolt but to un-
bolt the door of the oppressed : not to extinguish but to multiply and
realize their hopes. But alas! your Party turned for strength and success to slavery ; and so entirely identified itself with it that the
Party can live only in the life of the monster, and must die when
the monster dies. Hence it is that you are what you are. You
are stone-blind, both morally and politically. You see not God's
hand in this war. You see not that His time has at last come for
setting free his sable children. So deluded are you as to imagine
that pro-slavery will be popular forever and abolition unpopular
forever. But the Sun of the Seymours, and Rynders, and Woods
will soon set in darkness ; and the Sun of the Garrisons, and Phillips, and Cheevers will soon rise in splendor. Your spurious Democratic Party, deserted as it is by the Dickinsons and Butlers, and
by all who love country more than party, and freedom more than
slavery, will soon pass away, leaving History to tell on one of her
blackest pages of as base and wicked a Party as ever defied God
or trampled on man.

8th. In your infatuation you propose to cross swords with the
President—and this too not figuratively but literally. You threat-
en the forcible supplanting of the military power of the United
States by the merely civil power of this single State. This is
your way of standing by the President in his patriotic endeavors.
This is your way of standing by your country as she reels under
the blows of traitors — of traitors in arms and of more effective
traitors not in arms—of traitors in the rebellious States and of more

dangerous traitors in the loyal States. You say that the Union must be preserved. But your means for preserving it prove what kind of a Union it is that you are so intent on preserving. It is a Union for submission to the South. A Union for slavery and for the Democratic Party. You well know that our nation would have gone down very speedily had the civil power of Missouri, Kentucky and Maryland been allowed to override the military power of the nation. No man knows better than yourself to which side, but for the dread of that military power, the State, whose City shed Massachusetts blood would have gone, carrying with her both her civil and her military power. She might have gone South, even though opposed by a very large non-slavehold-ing majority.

To say that slavery is not the cause of the Rebellion is to say what is infinitely absurd. And yet for you to say it is any thing but strange. For you are a politician : and as all your political hopes are identified with slavery, you love it, cling to it, and are ever alert to screen it from blame. In consenting to let your idol be held responsible for this horrid Rebellion, you would consent to the only death you dread—your political death. Hence your queer theory that the Rebellion resulted from the characteristic differences between the people of New-England and the people of the Cotton States. I admit the existence of these differences. But who can not see that they have, in the main, proceeded from slavery? You imply that had there been as much homogeneous-ness between these peoples as is found " in the portions traversed by the great East and West lines of commerce," there would have been no Rebellion. I agree with you. But I bid you re-member that this is the homogeneousness of *anti-slavery* " por-tions". For save that one of these "lines" is partly in the skirts of the slaveholding section of the country, they all traverse States consecrated to Freedom, and only such. I thank you for this illustration of the homogeneousness and peacefulness of the anti-slavery "portions" of the country—for this illustration of the falseness of your position that an anti-slavery portion shares in the responsibility of the Rebellion. You further imply that had there been between the people of New-England and the people of the Cotton States the homogeneousness there is between the Border Free States and the Border Slave States, the Rebellion would not have been. You enumerate the causes, namely, "confluent rivers," etc. etc., to produce this homogeneousness; but you do not give facts to prove that it has been produced. There are none to give. How can there be facts to prove the homogeneousness of two peoples, one of whom holds the family relation sacred, and the other separates its members upon the auction-block?—among one of whom the laborer is counted to be worthy of wages, and among the other of whips?—among the native adult population of one of whom not a third can read, whilst in such population of the other the individual who can not read is a curiosity seldom to be met with? Homogeneousness between the Border Free and

Border Slave States! What imputation could be more insulting
to the former, and what more false in the face of the fact that,
whilst the Border Free States have furnished soldiers but to the
loyal army and these cheerfully and abundantly, the Border Slave
States, except little Delaware not so many, have furnished thousands—nay some, and probably each of them, tens of thousands—
of soldiers to the rebel army! There is not homogeneousness between Pennsylvania and Maryland; nor between Ohio, Indiana
and Illinois on the one hand and Kentucky on the other; nor between Iowa and Missouri. I admit that the people of Missouri are
coming to resemble the people of Iowa. But it is only because
Missouri is casting off slavery, and hasting to make her grand State
the grandest of perhaps all the States, and her City the Capital
of the Nation, whilst Washington is left to be the University of
the Nation. I admit that there is a class of men in the Border
Free States, and indeed in all the Free States, who are exceedingly homogeneous with a class of men in the Border Slave States.
I refer to the pro-slavery politicians in each section. Take for instance Governor Robinson of Kentucky and yourself. One might
be tempted to conclude that the same pen wrote your recent Message and his—so equally imbued are they with the pro-slavery
spirit; so equally devoted are they to the Border State policy,
which makes the saving of slavery paramount to the saving of
the country; and so equally determined are they that even in time
of war "the military is and must be subject to the civil authority,"
and must be made and kept so " at all hazards."

I ought to have said in its more proper connection, that such a
State as Ohio or Iowa will not thank you for implying that slavery
is less repugnant to her moral sense than to New-England's; and
that Western hatred of oppression is less radical than Eastern.

To bolster up this theory you say, (for this is your meaning, and
the only meaning that would be at all pertinent to the case,) that
the Border Free and Border Slave States came out as one at the
breaking out of the Rebellion. This is entirely true as regards
the former: — but it is glaringly false as regards the latter. Virginia went with the rebels; and for a long time there was a strong
doubt (not even yet wholly dispelled) whether there was not in
Maryland and also in Kentucky and Missouri a majority in favor
of going with the rebels. You are constrained to except " Eastern Virginia"—though you do it in a way so ingenious and artful,
that the careless reader would make scarce any account of the
exception. Nevertheless this " Eastern Virginia" is several times
as populous as the remainder of Virginia. And is it really so,
that you did not see that this exception, which you make, is fatal
to your attempt to prove that slavery is not the cause of the Rebellion? If you did not, then is there here another fact of the
stone-blindness which has come upon you. Why did Western
Virginia cast in her lot with the North? Because she has but half
a dozen thousand slaves, and wants to get rid of them. And why
did Eastern Virginia go with the South? Because she has several

hundred thousand slaves, and wants to hold and multiply them. Can you doubt that Eastern Virginia, had her slave population been as sparse as that of Western Virginia, would have come North? Can you doubt that Western Virginia, had hers been as dense as that of Eastern Virginia, would have gone South?

That the Western and Central *Free* States "enlisted warmly in a war for the Union and Constitution" I admit. But your implication that New-England did not is baldly and cruelly false. That the Administration has abandoned its "sole purpose to restore the Union and maintain the Constitution" is a slander. I had no part in bringing it into power, but not the less ready am I to do it justice. And if, as you substantially say, "the Central and Western States" have in this gloomy hour, when to stand by the country is to stand by the Administration, given the cold shoulder to the Administration, then it is the slanderers and not the slandered who are responsible for so calamitous an alienation. I charged you with slandering the Administration. The sole difference between Democrats, Republicans and Abolitionists at this point where you slander it, is that whilst all three agree that the one issue is the salvation of the Constitution and the Union, the Democrats are not willing to have them saved at the necessary sacrifice of slavery; the Republicans are; and the Abolitionists rejoice in the necessity.

To return for a moment to your queer theory. What will not a man do when he is in straits? You would not consent to the disgrace and ruin of your pro-slavery party, as you would do if you consented to have slavery held responsible for the accursed Rebellion. Hence your queer theory, that has not one fact nor one semblance of a fact to sustain it. The theory which is made from facts is valuable. But the theory to which facts are made is worthless. Emphatically worthless is yours, since you have not so much as taken the pains to coin facts, and have substituted for the coinage simple assertion!

Slavery not the cause of the Rebellion! Then why is it that, whilst every Free State came out instantly in battle array against the Rebellion, eleven of the Slave States embarked in it, and three, if not indeed all four, of the others gave only too abundant signs that they also would embark in it but for their fear of Federal troops? Slavery not the cause of the Rebellion! Then why is it that the rebels say it is?—and why is it that they insult the Civilization of the age by making slavery the boasted corner-stone of their new nation? — and by making the first of all the objects of their diabolical movement the protecting, spreading, and eternizing of slavery?

I do not murmur at the Providence, which has brought you again into high political power. On the contrary, I submissively accept it as a part of the penalty of the American people for their oppressions of the poor. Your election, instead of the election of the brave and noble man who rejoices in the deliverance of the slave and who with his three sons is in the army of his country

instead of being in the counsels of its foes, is, notwithstanding it
is so frightfully calamitous, to be endured as one of our merited
inflictions. Every nation prepares its own cup. We have made
ours very bitter. Nevertheless we must drink it. As a part of
the punishment for our unsurpassed crimes against humanity we
may have to witness the failure of all endeavors to save our beloved country, and may have to pass through the humiliation of
recognizing the Southern Confederacy. But God be praised that
over against all this deep and unutterable sorrow will be the deep
and unutterable joy that the slave is free! In spite of the influence of your Party to the contrary and of your individual and
amazing *determination* to the contrary, the slave will go free.
Yes, though the guilty nation, with whose continued existence
stands connected the highest object of your ambition, may be
left to perish, the innocent slave nevertheless shall surely go free.
Do you wonder at the positiveness with which I express myself
at this point? I answer that this being, high above all human
purposes and issues in it, a war of God against slavery, pro-slavery men are but fools in it, and only abolitionists competent to
advise in it, and foresee its grand results.

Faithful were the abolitionists, all through a quarter of a century, to warn their countrymen of this day of blood. But pro-
slavery politicians requited them with scorn. And so frenzied
are such politicians now, as to purpose to save the country by
crushing the abolitionists. This, however, is but as every impeni-
tently wicked people have dealt with their faithful prophets.

The counsels of the abolitionists — of the men who have made
slavery their life-long study — can alone, under God, save our
appallingly imperiled nation. Every step taken by her in accordance with these counsels is a step in the way of her salvation;
and her every step to the contrary is in the way to her destruction.

Your former and your present friend,

GERRIT SMITH.

STAND BY THE GOVERNMENT.

SPEECH IN ALBANY, FEBRUARY 27, 1863.

————•◆•————

After offering the following Resolution :

" Whereas, the one work of the nation is to crush the Rebellion ; and whereas it can be accomplished through the Government only : Therefore resolved, that Democrats, Republicans, and Abolitionists—men of all parties and men of no parties—should stand by the Government, and sympathize with it under its embarrassments, and bear its burdens, and be grateful for its fidelity, and, whilst quick to commend its wise measures, should never criticise its mistakes but in the spirit of patriotism instead of party, and but to make the Government stronger instead of weaker, and the enemy weaker instead of stronger."

Mr. Smith proceeded to say :
I am not rightly represented in all respects. For instance, because I am an old and zealous Temperance man, it is assumed that I am for having Government take the Cause of Temperance under its wing. Whereas the theory, which I have spent so much time during the last twenty years in elucidating and commending, is that Government has nothing to do with Churches nor even with Schools, with religious institutions nor even with moral reforms ; and that its only legitimate province is the narrow one of protecting the persons and property of its subjects. Hence when I would have Government shut up a dram-shop, it is not because I would have it enact a sumptuary law or care in the least for the cause of Temperance ; but it is solely because a portion of the men, who frequent that dram-shop, are wont to get crazed in it, and to go forth from it to perpetrate crimes against person and property. It is because that manufactory of madmen sends out one man to fire a dwelling, and another to murder a wife, and others to other deeds of mischief or horror. Then again because I am an old and radical Abolitionist, it is taken for granted that I would have our struggle to put down the Rebellion perverted

into a crusade against Slavery. Whereas ever since the Rebellion broke out, I have been entreating my countrymen not to fall away to any side issues, but to consecrate themselves "arm and soul" to the one work of putting down the Rebellion. Unceasingly have I summoned them to stand shoulder to shoulder in this work, notwithstanding their differences as Democrats, Republicans, and Abolitionists. To this end was my printed Letter in 1861 to Edwin Croswell. To this end have been many of my writings and speeches. With this struggle to put down the Rebellion I have from first to last been unconditionally identified. The President's blocking up of Fremont's and Hunter's Abolition way did not in the least diminish my devotion to the one absorbing purpose of putting down the Rebellion; and his Proclamation of Freedom could not increase it. Whether the Government in its changeful measures, was now for slavery or now against it, I kept steadily on in my zeal and labor for the overthrow of the Rebellion.

Excuse the egotism of these introductory remarks. I dislike egotism, whether it be in myself or in others. But I felt that I must make them in order to get your unprejudiced and open ears. I felt that you would not respect what I have to say to you, unless I should first disabuse you of your false impressions regarding my attitude toward the Rebellion.

The way is now open for me to mention some of our duties at this crisis.

1st. *The Rebellion must be put down.*

2d. *All hands must help put it down.*

The Republicans, Democrats, and Abolitionists must all help, be it at whatever risk to their respective parties. Indeed, so far as the Rebellion is concerned, they must all give up their parties, and become one party. Outside of this one party they may still maintain old party names and old party aims. But into this new and sacred party they must bring no party interests, no party jealousies, no party divisions. In this party all must be harmony; and its members must know each other only as Americans.

I add that whilst on the one hand the Abolitionists must help put down the Rebellion not merely because it is a Pro-Slavery one —(for, Slavery out of the question, they should be equally prompt to put it down)—on the other hand the Anti-Abolitionists must not withhold their help because it is a Pro-Slavery Rebellion. The Democrats must be as prompt to assist in putting down this Rebellion as they would be were it an Anti-Slavery one. They know that they would lose very little time in arraying (and that too most vindictively) all their might against a New-England Anti-Slavery Rebellion. They, who are now Peace Democrats, would then be War Democrats; and such of them, as are now the most tender to rebels, would then be the least patient with rebels.

I said that the Abolitionists must help put down the Rebellion. If any of them would not have it put down unless Slavery be put down with it or before it, they are wrong. The Rebellion is, aside from all questions of Slavery, an enormous evil; and, as such, all are bound to help suppress it, unconditionally and uncalculatingly. Moreover, in the light of a sound philosophy there is no right thing that *can* be damaged by ending an evil; and hence if the undertaking to abolish slavery be a right thing nothing is to be feared for it from the suppression of the Rebellion.

I called the existing Rebellion a Pro-Slavery one. I do not forget that there are persons who find it convenient to deny it that character. The Southern statesmen, one of whom calls Slavery the corner-stone of their new nation, do not thank these persons for this denial. The Southern clergymen will not thank them for it. They entirely concur with the Southern statesmen at this point. Their Bishops, in their recent Pastoral Letter, are not ashamed to avow that the Rebel States " are about to plant their national life" on Slavery.

3d. *The Northern people should all admit—nay, to use a more positive and proper word—they should all* DECLARE, *that the Rebellion is entirely groundless and exceedingly wicked.*

None among us should any longer say that the Abolitionists provoked the Rebellion. The saying of this goes if not to justify, nevertheless to excuse, the Rebellion; and it goes to reduce the hatred and horror of it, and also the strength of the purpose and endeavors to subdue it. I readily admit, that the Abolitionists did by their much talking and writing against Slavery greatly annoy the slaveholders. But surely this talking and writing, whether right or wrong, furnished no excuse for Rebellion. Free discussion is to be tolerated. If it is not, then the Missionaries, which our Churches have sent all over the heathen world to discuss idolatries and other forms of error, should be recalled; and then, indeed, the progress of mental and moral improvement, the earth over, should be arrested. Republicans and Abolitionists! will not you tolerate free discussion? I need not ask the Democrats whether they will. For, in the turn of things, they have become the champions of free speech. They, before whose frequent mobs against free speech I had twenty or thirty years ago to retreat and hide, have now become the loudest-mouthed defenders of free speech.

But you will perhaps say that the Abolitionists went beyond free discussion, and pushed up some of the Northern Legislatures to unconstitutional legislation against Slavery. But even if it was unconstitutional, it certainly gave no just occasion for Rebellion. If nothing else forbade Rebellion, it was forbidden by the fact that there was the Supreme Court of the United States to pass upon the constitutionality of the legislation and to make a decision that all would abide by. Right here, let me run a contrast between the North and the South for the purpose of taking all possible cavil and complaint at this point out of the mouth of the South. The whole South wrote or talked for Slavery. But it was only a small portion of the North which wrote or talked against it. Most of the Northern people either apologized for it, or absolutely defended it. Again, Southern men came North, and advocated Slavery in the broadest and most offensive terms. Nevertheless these Southern visitors were treated courteously and kindly. But when Northern men went South, they were, if however slightly suspected of being Abolitionists, insulted, frequently tarred and feathered, and not unfrequently murdered. And again whilst the North was entirely willing to have the question of the constitutionality of her Anti-Slavery legislation go to the Supreme Court, the South angrily and stubbornly refused to let her Pro-Slavery legislation undergo this trial. Such was the refusal of Charleston and New-Orleans, when Massachusetts sent Commissioners to those cities; and the Commissioners had instantly to turn homeward in order to avoid violence and death. And now, to continue the contrast, whilst the North, though under the provocation of these deep wrongs, did not rebel, nor even remonstrate, nor scarcely murmur ; the South, though suffering no wrong nor semblance of wrong, has rebelled, and armed herself against the nation. Nevertheless so debauched and blinded by Slavery had the North become, that, even in the face of this contrast, there are thousands amongst us who say and scores of thousands who believe, that the North and not the South is the aggressor—that the North is the guily injurer, and the South the injured and the innocent!

> " O judgment ! thou art fled to brutish beasts,
> And men have lost their reason !"

4th. The Rebellion must be put down unconditionally.
Government must make no conditions, and accept none. Stern, uncompromising, unrelenting must be its policy until the Rebellion is suppressed. After that, the freer the play of a merciful and fraternal spirit the more will my heart rejoice. Nor must any Republicans propose a Swiss mediator or any other mediator. Not must any Democrats recommend the disposing of the Rebellion by a Convention or popular Assembly to be held in Nashville, Louisville, or anywhere else. It is for Government, and Government only, to dispose of it. The people must not override their own Government. That is the most effectual way to disparage and destroy it. Our Government could never more be good for any thing after the people had taken the Rebellion out of its hands. Henceforth it would be a derision both at home and abroad ;—as contemptible, and probably as transient also, as a Mexican Government. Were a mob raging in your streets, would you leave it to the city of Troy to say what should be done with it ? Certainly not. Nor would you, instead of encouraging and strengthening your city government to disperse it, virtually get up another mob. This, however, you would do, should you, contemptuously thrusting aside your city government, summon the people to deal with the mob. Yes, in that case your people would be mobbing their own Government most

emphatically. Now, this Rebellion is but a mob—a mob on an extended scale ; and it is as exclusively the work of the Federal Government to put it down, as it is of a city government to put down a street mob; or of a father to put down the child who revolts against his authority.

I need not add that our Government will not tolerate Intervention, but will regard it as War;—and, this too, whether the Intervention be on the part of one nation or many nations ; under the plea of commerce or humanity.

5th. The Rebellion must be put down, let the consequences be what they may to the Constitution, the Union, or even to the country.

I have not said this to startle you, but to reconcile you to it. The nation must be reconciled to it, or perish. Suppose the revolting child I referred to should say : Father ! you had better not try to put me down. It might be the breaking up and ruin of the family." How prompt and proper would be the father's indignant answer : "Family or no family, you young rascal, you shall be put down." And down he'd put him, wholly irrespective of the bearing of the transaction upon the family. Nay, he would, as he ought to, entirely forget his family in his one absorbing purpose of subduing the rebel. Nevertheless in this forgetting of his family, he would best serve and most honor it.

Now, I hold that in just the spirit of this wronged and aroused father should the American people and American Government feel and act. Thus, more than any other wise, would America set an example full of glory to herself and of benefit to mankind. But if from her lack of an immovable resolution to exhaust herself, if need be, in conquering the diabolical Rebellion, it shall finally remain unconquered; then will America bring greater disgrace to herself and greater detriment to mankind than any other nation ever did. The lustre, which innumerable victories have shed upon the arms and name of England is infinitely less than would be that of her expending her last strength in crushing an utterly unprovoked and wicked revolt of a part of her counties. And that high-spirited nation would expend it, rather than give up her Government and her boundaries. Shame to you, English rulers, that you are not willing to have this nation also maintain Government and boundaries at whatever expense or hazard ! All honor to you English people, that you are coming out so bravely and so nobly against your rulers and for us at this point, which is so vital not only to us but to all mankind! And you do this too in the face of the arguments, that the giving up of our resistance to the Rebellion would give bread to your hungry ones. God bless these hungry ones for their patience and their sympathy with us, and for affording another shining instance that men of integrity " do not live by bread alone." The English masses, who have to confront aristocracy, can well sympathize with our brave armies, who have gone forth to battle with an aristocracy not less but more overbearing, and but little if any less mighty.

I add that the present is no time to talk, and get up issues and

2

multiply divisions, about the Constitution, the Union and the
country. One person may wish to have the Constitution altered,
and another may not. For one I do not, and never did, wish any
alteration in it. No Democratic stickler for *the Constitution as
it is*, be he living or dead, has ever spoken or written as much as I
have for *the Constitution as it is*. Two years ago the Democratic
Party and no small portion of the Republican Party were ready
for Pro-Slavery changes of the Constitution. I opposed them; but
I did not ask for Anti-Slavery changes. I was entirely content with
the Constitution just as the Fathers gave it to us. Again whilst one
person may wish the Union modified, another, like myself, may be
satisfied with its present terms. And again, whilst one person
may wish to have the country no larger, another may go as far as
I did in Congress, and wish to have it include Cuba and all Mexico.
Oh! no, the present is no time to agitate, or even to mention those
questions. There is time now for nothing else than for all of us
to band ourselves together, and to determine in the depths of
our soul, that the Rebellion shall go down, even though Constitution and Union and country go down with it. But some of you
will tell me, that you wish to save the Constitution, the Union and
the country. So do I wish to save them. There is, however,
only one way to save them; and that way is to forget them—to
forget them in the one engrossing purpose to crush the Rebellion.

Now does all this, which I have just been saying, seem extravagant? Nevertheless it is only in the spirit of all this that the
Rebellion can be overcome. It is this out-of-season talk for the
Constitution and the Union all the way through the war, that
has so confused the nation, and prevented the concentration of its
interest and energies at the point which claims all its interest and
energies; and that has done more than any and all things else to
demoralize, debase, and destroy the nation. If the Democrats,
Republicans, and Abolitionists would come into a mutual stipulation not to speak for ninety days of the Constitution, the Union
or Slavery, there would within that time grow up such an earnestness and unanimity in the work of annihilating the Rebellion,
that it would be annihilated.

"*The Constitution as it is and the Union as it was*"—this, all
the way through the War, has been the great motto, not of the
Democrats only but of most of the Republicans also. I do not
say that it was a bad motto with which to face the discontents,
murmurs, and threats that preceded the War. I do not say that
it was unwise in Mr. Lincoln and our statesmen generally to continue to recognize it, in those early stages of the war, which nearly all of us hoped would not result in actual and proper war.
But neither consistency nor any other consideration required them
to recognize it any longer. Its effect any longer could be but to
deceive and destroy. And yet, even now, when the strife has
taken on the dimensions of the widest war and the character of
the most horrid war, this motto is still current. Alas! what mis-
conceptions of the hour have they who, in this life-and-death-

struggle, would inspire us with any paramount anxiety, or indeed with any anxiety, for the Constitution and the Union! And, alas! how unfitted for a part in this struggle are all they who yield themselves up to this untimely and comparatively low inspiration! I say not that it will be improper to revive this motto after the rebels are conquered. But I do say that until then it should be buried and forgotten. For until then we have nothing to think of but the Rebellion, and nothing to do but to put it down.

A mobocratic spirit against the present charter and present boundaries of a city is beginning to show itself. The loyal citizens do well to meet this spirit with a motto, and to cry: " *The charter and the boundaries!*" But would not such a motto be madness after the mobocrats had already applied the torch and were already at work to reduce the city to ashes? It would be— and as emphatic madness is this prating about the Constitution and the Union in this fearful hour, when the mightiest Rebellion the world ever saw has raised the question—not what will become of a Paper and of politics, but what will become of our wives and children. " *Death to the mobocrats!*" could be the only suitable motto in the one case, as " *Death to the rebels!*" is the only suitable one in the other.

Oh! no, this is not, as it is still claimed to be by the designing and the deluded, " *a War to maintain the Constitution and restore the Union.*" In its beginning it may have been proper to call.that the issue. But it is no longer so, now that the Rebellion has reached its present proportions, and is so full of peril to the very life of the nation.

In this connection I would rebuke the frequent question — whether we mean to subjugate the Southern States. Until the Rebellion is subdued we mean to do nothing but subdue it. After that will be soon enough to decide what to do after that. To decide it now would be but to embarrass us, and to get up another issue on which to divide us. For the present we are to see to it, that the South do not subjugate us.

6th. *This clamor for carrying on the War in only a Constitutional way should cease — for it springs neither from good sense nor from an enlightened and enlarged patriotism, and it is fraught with peril if not indeed with ruin to our cause.*'

It is not true that we are bound to carry on the war Constitutionally at all hazards. I know that the rebels who have kicked aside the Constitution say that we are. This was the burden of Breckinridge's speeches in the Senate just before he left it to join the rebel army. But to say that we are to receive the advice of the rebels with caution, is not to treat them discourteously or ungratefully. Their professed regard for the Constitution and for our welfare through an incessantly scrupulous and minute observance of it is certainly not above reasonable suspicion.

I admit that I see no necessity for violating the Constitution in carrying on the War. But if I did I would not hesitate to have it violated. I totally deny that this nation or any other nation is

to regard itself as tied up to a Paper in the prosecution of war.
Never before was there a nation so insane as to maintain for one
moment the idea that, in a life-and-death-struggle, it was bound at
whatever risk to take those steps and those only which had been
marked out for it in a time of peace and safety. What the salvation of the nation calls for is to be done, whether the Constitution does or does not provide for it. The person who says otherwise, would be like to evince more concern to save the hat than
the head of the drowning man. "All that a man hath will he
give for his life"—and all that a nation hath, Constitution in-
cluded, should she be willing to give for her life. The country is
more than the Constitution. Not for the sake of the Constitution
may the country be hazarded—but for the sake of the country
the Constitution may be sacrificed. And I repeat that the putting
down of the rebels is more than both Constitution and country.

There is, my hearers, a better inheritance than a Constitution
or even than a country, which we can leave to our successors.
This better inheritance is the glorious and immortal fact, that we
made more account of putting down an internal Rebellion than
we did of preserving our treasure or our life, our Constitution or
our country. To resist high-handed and bloody crime at whatever hazard or expense to ourselves, and to be less concerned to
escape from death than from deep and enduring disgrace—surely
this will be more precious in the esteem of our children than any
thing we could have saved for them by failing of this fidelity and
bravery, and going down to the low grounds of calculation and
compromise. To be willing to fling away our all in withstanding
the assaults of a demonized gang on the sacred edifice of free government—this is to make ourselves the greatest blessing to those
who shall come after us ; and this is to do more toward carrying
upward and onward the human family than could be done by
saving a thousand countries in which this sublime spirit of self-
sacrifice is not found.

I said that I see no necessity for violating the Constitution in
carrying on war. The paper withholds no needed power. It
provides that Congress may declare war and enact all laws "necessary and proper" to give effect to the declaration. Congress
is, of course, the sole judge as to what laws are "necessary and
proper." Surely here is power enough.

We must all stand by the Government, and do all we can to
make strong its heart and hands. Ours is an intelligent Government, and it is honestly intent in putting down the Rebellion.
Every government falls into mistakes. Doubtless ours has fallen
into some. But the Democrats complain too unqualifiedly and
sweepingly of it. I admit that they are entirely right in denouncing the unnecessary seizure and imprisonment of citizens.
Nevertheless there *are* instances of their necessary seizure and
imprisonment ; and moreover there are instances (I confess comparatively few) where there is not opportunity for the examina-
tion of the accused either previous to or immediately after his

arrest. But, Democrats, if you will bear in mind that this power
to seize and imprison citizens is, although a very necessary one, a
very odious one, you will see that Government is under a strong
motive to exercise it sparingly, and only for the safety of the
country. I am not a member of the Republican Party. Nevertheless I can trust our Republican Government at this point. I
would, Democrats, that you also might be willing to trust it.
Enlighten it, and remonstrate with it, as there may be occasion.
But do not array yourselves against it. For the dear country's sake,
be on its side—its friend and not its foe.

Let me speak of an error, which not Democrats only but Republicans also are liable to fall into. Now a Fremont, now a
Hunter, now a Fitz-John Porter, and now a McClellan comes
under the censure of the Government. Perhaps in every instance
the censure is unjust. But, Democrats and Republicans, if there
be an instance in which you are entirely sure it is unjust, nevertheless do not add to the embarrassments of the Government and
the perils of the country by making it an occasion for compliment-
ing and glorifying the censured one. In this wise you will gather
a party around him, and it will not fail to be a party against the
Government. But the Government, so long as it has the armed
South for a party against it, can not afford to encounter any other
party. I do not know but the Government fell into mistakes in
regard to all these Generals. But I do know that whether it did
or did not, the present is not the time to punish the mistakes of
the Government. As much as we can now do is to punish the
crimes of the rebels. Let the friends of the Fremonts and Mc-
Clellans be patient. Justice will be done to their favorites; and
the less hurriedly the more perfectly.

I pass to the wrong which those Abolitionists commit, who condemn the President for not proclaiming freedom to all the slaves,
and also to the wrong which those Democrats commit, who condemn him for proclaiming it to any. Now the truth on the one
hand is, that the President has no right to abolish Slavery except as
Commander-in-Chief, and no right even in that capacity to abolish
it any further or faster than the military necessities of the country
call for. The truth on the other hand is, that he has the right to
abolish any and all Slavery the abolition of which is called for by
such necessities. In his much criticised, much condemned, and
much ridiculed Letter to Horace Greeley the President laid down
the true doctrine in this case. If it would help us in the War to
call to our side the slaves of South-Carolina, then the President
should call them. If it would not help us to call those of North-
Carolina, those he should not call. In nothing of all this has he
aught to do with the morality of Slavery. I grant that if the
slaves will not come, it is useless to call them; and I am aware
that it is very frequently and confidently asserted that their love
of their masters and mistresses is too great to permit them to
come. If, however, they will come, then by all means they should
be called — and this too even if they should, as it is said they

would, prove too lazy to work where there are no whips to work
under; and even if they should, as it is said they would, prove
too cowardly to fight. For left where they are their toil sustains
the Rebellion.

I claim not to know whether the slaves will come to our standard—nor whether, if they should come, they will either work or
fight. But I do claim that, inasmuch as there is a chance, be it
however small, that they will come, and a chance, be it however
small, that they will work, and a chance, be it however small, that
they will fight, the President's Proclamation of Freedom is justified. For what, if it shall turn out that the slaves *are* able to
tear themselves away from their dear masters and mistresses!
What an immense advantage to our cause will that be; and even
though they shall prove unable or unwilling to render us any service after coming to us! And then if it shall turn out that they
are willing to work on our side, and to work as faithfully as did
that comparative handful of escaped and deserted slaves who,
instead of being, as was all along alleged, a charge upon our national treasury, put into it, over and above wages and expenses,
between five and six hundred thousand dollars—then will this
immense advantage be doubled. And then a still greater advantage to our cause if they shall be willing to fight for it, and our
officers and soldiers shall be so earnestly patriotic as to let them
fight for it. For I know not why, if they shall be willing to fight
for us, they shall not fight with as signal bravery and effective-
ness as did the negroes in both of our wars with Great Britain.
Whether our officers and soldiers will be so much in earnest to
put down the Rebellion as to let the despised negroes help them
put it down, remains to be seen. If *entirely* in earnest, they would
welcome the aid not only of negroes and Indians, but of even the
devil himself.

I repeat that I know not whether the slaves will come to us, or
whether if they do they will work or fight. They are called the
most patient and forgiving of all the races. They will certainly
prove that they are, if they can forget that monstrous and meanest
crime of letting the thousands, who toiled on the Vicksburgh cut-
off, fall again into the hands of the vindictive slaveholders; and
if they can also forget the innumerable instances in which slaves
coming to our lines, some with very valuable news of the designs
and movements of the enemy, and all with hearts and hands to
help us, have with satanic malignity been returned to the fate
from which they had fled; and if, in a word, they can forget our
persistent ridicule, loathing and murderous hate of a people, who
have done not one wrong in return for the mountains of wrong
under which we have buried them. It is true that even such a
people may at last be goaded to revengeful and bloody insurrections. Not, however, if they can have a way of escape from their
oppressors. The President's Proclamation is the safety-valve.
One of my chief reasons for welcoming it was that it would probably prevent servile insurrections.

I said that the Proclamation is to be justified in the light of even the least favorable expectations from it. But should we realize from it all this, which I have been speaking of as possible, then should we all rejoice in it. Should we hear to-night that a Southern black regiment has overcome a rebel white one, would we not all swing our hats? Would not even the Democrats? It would indeed put to shame some of their oftenest repeated and most confident predictions, and it would take from their harp its most available string. But, Democrats, you would be too patriotic and magnanimous to mind that—wouldn't you?

I spoke of the blacks coming to our side. Let me not be misunderstood. The abolition of Slavery will not send the Southern blacks to the North, but it will send the Northern blacks to the South. A genial climate, and, still more, masses of their race will attract them thither. They who seek to make the white laborer of the North jealous of abolition, do so either very ignorantly or very disingenuously.

And there is still another complaint which I have to make. It is the injustice and insult to the President of which they are guilty, who charge him with turning the war into an abolition war. He solemnly declares that his sole end is to put down the Rebellion; and that whatever he does with Slavery is done but incidentally, and but to that sole end. What, if the President, having taken it into his head that one of the most effective things which could be done toward prostrating the Rebellion is to free the cotton from the tenacious grasp of the Confederate Government, should be multiplying endeavors to that end? Would it be fair to charge him with perverting the war into a war to free the cotton? I deliberately affirm that it would be quite as fair as to charge him with perverting it into a war to free the slave. Let us all be just to the President. To be unjust to him is not only to wrong him, but to wrong and perhaps ruin the country. Democrats! there are some who accuse you of opposing the President's Proclamation, because you would pervert the war into a war for Slavery. Are you not indignant at the accusation? Surely, you should be. For nothing in all the history of man could be more revolting than such a perversion of a just war, and such a betrayal of a righteous cause. Great is the wickedness of a slaveholding people who make war for Slavery. But the wanton and unmitigated wickedness of a non-slaveholding people, who should join them, is infinitely greater.

I must bring my speech to a close. Do you wonder that I, so old and so radical an Abolitionist, have expressed in it no concern about Slavery? I could not express what I did not feel. Since the bombarding of Sumter I have felt no concern about Slavery—for I could not doubt that it was the effectual bombarding of Slavery. As the war has advanced I have been increasingly confident that the people would never consent to reëstablish the cause of all this blood and horror and desolation. As I have seen the plowshare of war pass through Slavery, I have felt more and more that the time for the abomination to pass away had come. And now have we signs that the very earthquakes of war will soon be rending this mountain of oppression, and tossing its parts hither and thither beyond all possibility of restoration.

Moreover, civilization is everywhere casting off Slavery; and there is reason to hope that even the South will become so far civilized by this war as no longer to desire Slavery. It is indeed sad to have to number war amongst the civilizing agents. Nevertheless so it is, that whilst the nations are on their present low plane—a plane in the case of some of them not above the barbarism of slaveholding—it is hardly extravagant to say of them that, " without shedding of blood there is no " civilization. War is emphatically the wörst of all remedies. But the nations are still too low and barbarous to try only the better ones.

Yes, the slave is soon to go free. Heaven's time for setting him free is at hand; and earth and hell can not prevail against heaven. He goes free by the shedding of blood. But it is the blood of his common oppressors North and South, instead of his own. Wondrous manifestations of the Divine hand! Wondrous retributions of the Divine justice!

But though I am sure that the innocent slave shall go free, I am not sure that the guilty nation shall live. God alone knows what penalty will be adequate to its enormous, continued, and unrepented of crimes against his poor. Perhaps it is to be destroyed, and to be a warning, loud and long, against oppression. Nevertheless, though we are to be submissive to whatever may be in store for her, we are to labor zealously, wisely, and incessantly for her salvation.

My hearers, we will all stand by the Government—will we not? Although some of us are Democrats and some Republicans and some Abolitionists, we will nevertheless lock hands as Americans— will we not? We will all of us, notwithstanding our party divisions and party interests, generously and patriotically band ourselves together to crush this causeless and accursed Rebellion— will we not? Would that we might this night feel more deeply than ever that it is not by the rebels that we can be conquered, but only by ourselves. Nothing is truer than that the life of the Rebellion is in disunion at the North. Nothing is truer than that it would find its death in union at the North.

Ere taking my seat, let me remind you of our duty to stand by our Army—by the brave men who have gone out from among us to suffer every hardship and to face every peril in the high and holy work of suppressing the most nefarious of all conspiracies. But the way to stand by them is to stand by the Government they serve. To desert the Government is to desert them. Our soldiers bid us stand by the Government. They are afflicted that so many of us do not. They are indignant at the divisions by which we encourage the foe, and make him abler to drive back and slaughter our friends. Such heartlessness toward themselves as well as toward the country is very unlike that reward of sympathy, gratitude, and love on which they counted when they went forth to fight her battles. Our slain soldiers, could they speak, would bid us stand by the Government. Our tens of thousands of broken families weeping over those who went to the army never more to return from it, bid us stand by the Government. The enlightened friends of freedom and righteousness the earth over bid us stand by the Government. And, loud above all, comes down the voice out of heaven: "Stand by the Government! Stand by the Government!"

DENYING SUFFRAGE EVEN TO SOLDIERS!

TELL the drunkard or the debauchee that he is a ruined man, and he will stare upon you with astonishment and frown upon you with indignation. So is it with this nation. She is annoyed and angry at the charge of being ruined. Nevertheless she has been ruined for more than forty years. From the sad hour when Slavery triumphed over Freedom in the Missouri Compromise, down to the present no sadder hour she has never ceased to be a ruined nation.

Our nation saw a fierce and mighty Rebellion spring up within her borders and ripen into the organization of an independent government. She saw here and there her little peace army, or rather armed police, betrayed into its hands; and here and there the rebels plundering her treasuries. She saw them so bold as to fire at her ships, and seize her forts, and build up fortifications over against her own. Nevertheless (thing unheard of in the history of nations!) she did not move. Why did she not? Simply because she could not. Why could she not? Simply because she was ruined.

It is true that the news of the taking of Sumter proved that the nation was not entirely dead. This electric shock detected some lingering remains of patriotism. But that President Lincoln, though loyal and loving the right, was nevertheless incompetent to avail himself of the occasion and to strike effectively for her salvation, was among the painful proofs that the nation was still ruined. In common with the nation, he was drugged and debauched by Slavery. How then could he suddenly rise up in earnest resistance to the Rebellion it had prompted? Oh! could he have then believed that the military necessities of the country would justify his summoning to his standard every slave in the land, how soon would the Rebellion have been put down! Or even had he gone no farther than to summon to it, at that nick of time, the slaves of the revolted States. Are we told that the people were not yet prepared for so strong a measure? They were: and never since so well. Moreover, the measure itself would have completed the preparation—would have supplied any possible lack in it. Nothing is so mighty to convert men to the right as bravery for the right. The fearless and unhesitating leader is the one they love to follow. Had the tide in our nation's affairs been taken at the Sumter flood it would have led her " on to fortune." But our

GERRIT SMITH ON THE REBELLION. 27

leader lacked the courage and decision to take it. Through his timidity and indecision it was left to subside, with but little profit having come of it. And alas, how has her voyage since been "bound in shallows and in miseries!" The enthusiasm kindled by the outrageous and infamous assault on Sumter was suffered to pass away. Very soon the people sank down into a willingness to hear demagogues and traitors prate about the Constitution. 'In none but a ruined nation can the people, at the very time when the life of their nation is struck at, give ear to such prating.

Does this late-in-the-day call upon the blacks to enroll themselves in our army prove that our nation is not ruined? Far from it—especially so, since the Government has not the manliness to promise to see to it that captured blacks shall, instead of being murdered or sold into Slavery as the rebels threaten, be treated as prisoners of war.

I referred to this prating about the Constitution. It continues unabated to this day. Anxiety lest we may lose, not the Country, but the Constitution, is no less irrational and is infinitely more ruinous than would be anxiety to save, not the man from drowning, but his hat from going down stream.

I, who have never spoken or written one word against the Constitution, and who have spoken and written more words for it than did ever any Pro-Slavery man living or dead, can afford to say that this prating for it has made "Constitution" the most offensive of all the sounds that strike upon my ear. "Slavery" itself is to me a less disturbing word than this one under cover of which Slavery is hypocritically served.

I spoke of the continuance of this prating. In reply to every proposition for a more vigorous prosecution of the war, we are still met with the cry: "The Constitution! The Constitution!!" And even now, when we would help on the war by allowing the soldiers of the State of New-York to vote at her elections, we are met by this same cry. Surely, surely, we have here another proof that our nation is ruined.

How commanding are the reasons for allowing them to vote! No other class of men have so emphatic a right to vote for the rulers of their country as these, who are periling their lives for her and doing more than any and all other classes to save her. There is no other class of men whose rights we should hold so sacred. Then to convince them that we love them and stand by them, we should hasten to recognize all their rights and to facilitate their exercise. Moreover, that they may be inspired to do their utmost for their country they must see that they are regarded, not as her armed defenders only, but as still her citizens—and her citizens not robbed of, but protected in, their rights by their fellow-citizens whom they have left at home. A European army is for the most part made up of the dregs of the population—of men without acknowledged political rights and without character. Very different is our army. It is composed of those, who, besides being our superiors in patriotism and courage, are our equals in rights,

intelligence, and character. Let this be borne in mind by all who
would disfranchise them. I add that there is no other class of
men, whom we should feel ourselves so strongly bound to honor
and to gratify in every possible way as our noble and beloved
soldiers. Another argument for allowing the soldiers to vote is,
that here one of them who is a Democrat and there one of them
who is a Republican will, under some excuse or other, go home
to play his part in deciding a hotly contested and doubtful election. This, besides damaging the efficiency of the army, furnishes
just ground of complaint, now to one of the parties and now to
the other. Nevertheless the temptation to this violation of duty
is too strong to be successfully resisted by all. American citizens, educated, as they are, to prize the ballot, and accustomed,
as they are, to cast it, can not easily school themselves into content-
ment with not casting it.

But it is claimed that the framers of the Constitution of our
State intended that voting at our elections should be always in
person and never by proxy. Our Pro-Slavery demagogues have
made so much account of the Pro-Slavery words of some of the
framers of the Federal Constitution, that the habit of interpreting
a Constitution in the light of what its framers intended has come
to obtain all over the country. But in point of fact the intentions
of its framers as such are not to be allowed to enter at all into the
interpretation and meaning of a Constitution—no, no more than
the intentions of the scrivener, who wrote the deed, into the
interpretation and meaning of the deed. What the people who
adopted it intended by it is the only legitimate inquiry at this
point: and what they intended by it is to be learned solely from
its letter where that is unambiguous. , Nay more—where the purpose is to defeat rights (and suffrage is among the highest rights)
we are not at liberty to seek help outside of the letter of the Constitution.

The letter of the Constitution in the case before us is entirely
free from ambiguity. It clearly leaves it to the Legislature to
say how the voting shall be—whether in person or by proxy—
whether it shall be all in one way—or a part in one way, and a
part in another. It does say that a part of the voting shall be by
ballot: and it might as easily have said that all voting shall be in
person. But it does not say it. What it would have said, had it
spoken on the point, is an utterly impertinent inquiry. Moreover,
it is a fair, not to say irresistible inference that inasmuch as the
Constitution does at one point and only one point prescribe the
manner of voting, it intended to leave it to the Legislature to prescribe it at every other. I add that were it our custom to vote
by proxy no one would regard such voting as repugnant to the
Constitution. But clearly if with that custom it would not be unconstitutional, the lacking of that custom can not make it unconstitutional. Not custom, but the Constitution, determines what
voting is Constitutional.

So far as the Constitution is concerned the Legislature may

provide that all the voting be by proxy. I admit that such a provision would be unwise. I admit too that I can conceive of no other case than that of the soldiers in which it would be wise. In their case it would be, not only for the reasons I have mentioned, but because the soldiers are so numerous. I would not, for the sake of accommodating a comparative handful of aged or infirm men, have our States allow so objectionable a mode of voting as is that by proxy. But for the sake of securing the rights of half a million to a million of soldiers I would not only have them allow it, but I would denounce the denial of it as unreasonable and unrighteous—a high crime against both the soldiers and the country.

For one I shout with joy, and I would have every other lover of his dear country and of her dear defenders do so, that there is not one line nor one word in our State Constitution against voting by proxy.

I said that our nation is ruined. She is. But I have never despaired of her recovery from her ruin. Few things inspire me with so strong a hope of this recovery as the growing disposition to let the army vote. They who meet the rebels face to face, know better how to vote than do we who keep ourselves at a safe distance from the foe. Ay, and they have better earned the right to vote. If either of us must be disfranchised—I, who remain amidst the comforts and safety of home, or he who welcomes the sufferings and perils of the soldier; I, who know the rebels but by hearing of them, or he, who knows them by seeing and feeling them; I, who but read of the battles, or he, who has part in them—then, in the name of reason and religion, it should be I and not he. GERRIT SMITH.

PETERBORO, April 20th, 1863.

SPEECH AT LOYAL LEAGUE CONVENTION

IN

UTICA, MAY 26TH, 1863.

———◆———

THIS strikes me as a very mottled assemblage, politically considered, and in a certain point of view, morally considered also. Here we are, Democrats and Republicans, temperance men and anti-temperance men, some one thing and some another, and there are soldiers among us. I see soldiers [applause] who have returned from the battle-field wet with the sweat of war, and some of them with its blood. They have returned to receive our benedictions and to be the witnesses of our enduring and deep gratitude for their heroic defense of our bleeding country. [Applause.] Now, what is the object that has had the power to collect this heterogeneous assemblage? I answer, it is a common cause. This is the mighty loadstone that has been able to draw us together, in spite of our mutual differences, in spite of our different views and different character. There are persons so bigoted and so impracticable as not to consent to come into a common cause. I know Democrats who, not even to save their beloved country— I can not say, however, how beloved to them—[laughter]—there are Democrats, I say, who not even to save this dear country, will consent to vote any other than a Democratic ticket; and I know Republicans who will not consent to vote any other but a Republican ticket; and I know Abolitionists, and I am ashamed of them, [laughter,] and even temperance men, who will not consent to work with any other than their own sort of people. But we, I thank God for it, are not such. We, though differing from each other at many points, can, nevertheless, when the nation calls for it, consent to work together. Now, I ask, what is this common cause which has drawn us together? Just here give me your special attention. I ask again, what is this common cause? Is it to save the Constitution? Oh! it is inexpressibly more than that. There are many good, patriotic men, who don't wish the Constitution saved as it is; they wish to have it altered. I, for one, would not have one word of it altered; I have pleaded for it with lips and pen, more than any Democrat, living or dead. I would not have one word in it altered. [Applause.] Well, if this common cause is not to save the Constitution, is it to save the Union? Oh! no, unspeakably more than that. There are good men, and wise men, who do not like all the terms of our Union; I like them all. [Applause.] I have never taken in my life, with lips or pen, the slightest exception to any of them; and probably never shall. Well, is it, then, the saving of the country that is this common cause? It is not even that, for there are many good men who do not like the present boundaries of our country. They wish it to be made smaller. For my own part, every rood of it is dear to my heart. [Applause.] I would not have one star pass from the National flag. [Applause.] Not even poor South-Carolina. [Applause and laughter.] I love even South-Carolina. I love her for the memory of her noble men who stood by the side of our Revolutionary fathers. I love her for another reason; I love her for what she will become again when she shall have come out of her present degeneracy and madness. Well, now, if this common cause which has drawn us together is not the saving of the Constitution, nor the saving of the Union, nor the saving of the country, pray what, then, is it? My answer will be—and it will leap up from all your hearts to your lips—it is the putting down of this accursed and causeless Rebellion. [Applause.] That is the common cause that has drawn us together. And now, mark you, we all stand together at this point, where all good, and just, and patriotic men can and do stand with us. [Applause.] And then one thing more: that is the very point where unpatriotic and selfish men refuse to stand with us. The very point. And yet, some of these unpatriotic and self-seeking men, and traitors among them, are very eager to assure us of their intense regard for the Union and Constitution and country. But when we turn upon them with the question, "Are you for putting down the Rebellion?" they are found wanting. That is just the only test to apply to them, and under its application they fail. I recollect that more than thirty years ago, when Great Britain was agitated by the proposition to abolish British slavery, some Quakers supplied themselves with an image of a kneeling slave, and the appealing question running out of its mouth: "Am I not a man and a brother?" When the candidates for seats in Parliament would come round to these Quakers and solicit their votes, and tell them of the many fine things they would do if elected — things peculiarly acceptable to Quakers—these cunning Quakers would thrust in the face of these candidates this appealing image, and ask of them: "Can you go that? If you can't go that, we can't go you." Just so do we deal with these men, when they prate about their love for the Constitution, the Union, and the country. I ask them, and you ask them, can you go for putting down the Rebellion? If you can't go that, we can't go you. Oh! why should we go these vile hypocrites—for such they are—who talk about being for the Constitution, and the Union, and the country, and yet go not for putting down the Rebellion, the putting down of which can alone save these blessings to us, and the triumph of which will rob us of

32 GERRIT SMITH ON THE REBELLION.

them all? And now we have before us but one duty; our one
work is the work of putting down the rebellion. You have got to
come to this point. I don't allow myself to be a co-worker with
any one on earth who does not come to this point. The putting
down of this Rebellion must be done, come what will to Constitution and Union, and even country. [Applause.] Can you go
that? [Applause and cries of "Yes, yes."] For I hold that our
duty to Justice, and putting down this Rebellion, is infinitely
more commanding and absolute than any duty we owe to the
Constitution or the Union, or even the boundaries of our country.
I claim that we are to go for putting down the Rebellion unconditionally. Can you go that? You are not to say, we will consent
to put down the Rebellion on condition of the saving of the Constitution, the saving of the Union, or the saving of the country.
You are to say, we go for putting down the Rebellion unconditionally; and that is just where these traitorous enemies will not
go along with us. [Applause.] What!—some one questions
me—would you go for putting down this Rebellion with all the
possible risks that the Union, the Constitution, and the country
might go down with it? I answer, I would. I answer, I make
no calculation at all at that point. My only duty has been, from
the first, the putting down of this Rebellion. And here, some old
Abolitionists, perhaps, would ask me: Do you go for putting
down this Rebellion at all possible hazards, that Slavery may
survive and be stronger than ever? I do. I run that risk.
[Applause.] I have no conditions to make in behalf of any of
my hobbies, and have not had since the day the news reached me
at Peterboro of the bombardment of Sumter. [Applause.] And
now let me here say, that in my philosophy, the putting down of
crime can not bring any harm to any good—can not bring any
help to any evil. Hence the putting down of this rebellion, which
is the crime of crimes, can not bring any possible harm to any
good, in the Constitution, in the Union, or in the country, or in
Freedom—none whatever. I call it the crime of crimes. Earth
has never known a greater crime than this attempt to destroy a
nation which had never done any thing to provoke that attempt—
a nation which had always been not only just, but exceedingly
partial, to those guilty of this piratical and murderous attempt.
[Applause.] And now let me here say, that to make ourselves
most effective in this work, we ought to cultivate earnestness.
Oh! what an immense advantage the South has had over us in
that respect! If all our early Generals—I beg your pardon, Mr.
President, I didn't include yourself—[laughter]—you are too
nearly kindred to me that I should do that—I say if our early
Generals had had but a tithe of the earnestness that charac-
terizes the South and Southern Generals, we should not have
needed to be meeting here; the Rebellion would long ago have been
ended. And there is one thing more we need to cultivate, and
that is resentment. Can you go that? ["Yes, sir," and applause.] I know there is a sentimental, namby-pamby religion,

which takes fright at the idea of cultivating resentment. We need more resentment to fight the rebels as we ought to fight them. That has been our want all the way through. I recall a conversation with that great and good man, Theodore Parker, which I had a few years before his death—a conversation on the elements in human character. He claimed great credit for our power of hearty hating. That's like him ; and were he now alive, you might be sure of having at least one hearty hater of the Rebel. lion. He would exclaim with the Psalmist : "Do not I hate them, O Lord! that hate thee? I hate them with a perfect hatred." Perhaps some one would remind me of the prayer : " Father, forgive them, they know not what they do." Now, I hold that this resentment is entirely compatible with the highest civilization and purest Christianity, and entirely consistent with forgiveness ; but, moreover, (these rascals *do* know what they do. [Great laughter and applause.] Our Saviour had none such in his eye when he prayed. [Applause.] They know what they do, and they do it with a hatred and with a will that puts to shame our indecision and gentleness. I say we must go unconditionally for putting down the Rebellion. And let me add, our loyalty is to be unconditional. We have tried our Government and we can trust it. [Applause.] I do not say that we are bound to agree with it in all its views of tariffs and other things ; I do not say that we are bound to approve all its war measures even. It is entitled to our loyalty, because it has abundantly proved itself to be honestly and earnestly intent on putting down the Rebellion. I observed this forenoon a skittishness on one point—at the point of politics. A word on that. I have observed, I meant to say, that some persons are afraid that this grand Loyal League, into which I would have all right men of the North, South, East, and West enter, will become a party machine. Now, I would have this grand Loyal League a mighty power in politics. That's my view of it. [Applause.] I would have it work day and night to keep out of political office every man who is not unconditionally against the Rebellion. I do not say to keep out of office Democrats or Republicans, but every man who does not stand by the Government—who is not unconditionally for the Government. I have never in my life voted a Republican ticket ; for I am, as I think, a Democrat of Democrats. Not a sham, spurious Democrat ; but a man going for the equal rights of all men. [Applause.] If any man here can say, "I am a Democrat," I answer in Paul's words : " I, more." Our great work is before us. It is not to save the Union, or the Constitution, or the country ; that is all prating. I do not want to hear a man speak about his love for his country, but rather about his hatred of the rebels. I will infer his love for his country from his hatred of the rebels. Put down the rebellion, and the Union, and the Constitution, and the country will take care of themselves. If a murderer should be discovered in Utica, the concern is to be, not for the safety of Utica, but to arrest and punish the murderer. Arrest and punish him, and Utica will take

3

care of herself. Nor do I want you to talk about what shall be
done after the Rebellion is put down. The Rebellion is not put
down yet, and we never shall put it down if we allow ourselves
to be diverted from the actual and urgent duties of the present to
speculations in regard to the future. The only problem, Mr. President, that we can solve to-day, is putting down the Rebellion. I
would postpone every other thought to that solution. Let me
add, " sufficient to the day is the evil thereof." We must grudge
nothing ; we must grudge no help, no precious treasure, no precious
lives. Neither treasure nor life would be worth any thing to us,
or any right-minded man, if this Rebellion were triumphant.
If we should fail, we shall need no property to live on, for then
we shall be sinking under loads of infamy and anguish of heart,
and shall desire to live no longer. [Applause.]

SPEECH ON THE REBELLION AND THE DRAFT

IN

OSWEGO, JULY 29TH, 1863.

———•◦•———

I AM embarrassed at the very outset. For I recollect that I am an abolitionist; and I recollect that in the public esteem he who is an abolitionist can not be a patriot. How then can I get a hearing from you? For surely you are not willing to hear any other than a patriot on National affairs. I must propitiate you if I can. I will try the power of a confession to that end. My confession is—that if a man can not be a patriot whilst yet an abolitionist,·he should cease to be an abolitionist — that he should renounce his abolition if it at all hinders him from going for his country. I add that I go no longer for the Anti-Slavery Society, nor for the Temperance Society, no nor for my Church, if they go not for my country.

But what is it to go for one's country? Is it to go for her right or wrong? It is not. The true man goes for nothing in himself that is wrong. The true patriot goes for nothing in his country that is wrong. It is to go for all her boundaries, and to yield up no part of them to her enemy. It is to be unsectional—and to know no North and no South, no East and no West. It is to go for the unbroken and eternal union of all her sections. It is to love her with that Jewish love of country, which takes pleasure in her very stones and favors even the dust thereof. How very far then is he from going for his country who would surrender a part of her to appease the men who have rebelled against her! And let me here say that he does not go for her who, for the sake of securing the abolition of slavery, would consent to dismember her. Another way for going for one's country is to cling to her chosen form of government—in a word, to her Constitution. I do not mean that it is to prate for her Constitution and to affect a deep regard for it, whilst sympathizing with its open enemies—ay, and to affect this regard for the very purpose of thereby more effectively serving those enemies. It is, as in our case who have so excellent a Constitution, sincerely to value and deeply to love its great principles of justice, liberty and equality—those very principles which caused the Southern despots to make war upon it and fling it away — those very principles which caused the Northern sympathizers with these despots to hate it in their hearts whilst yet their false lips profess to love it. To go for one's country is also to make great account of her cherished names and of all that is precious in her institutions, traditions, and memories. But of all the ways of going for one's country that of going against her enemies is at once the most effective and the most evidential of sincerity and earnestness.

Let us glance at some of our duties in this crisis.

In the first place, we are to stand by the Government. Not to stand by it is not to stand by the country. Were the Government unfaithful I would not say so. But it is faithful. It is intent on saving the country. And it is not the weak Government which it is accused of being. In both Houses of Congress the cause of the country has many able advocates. There are strong men in the Cabinet. The President is himself a strong man. His Pro-Slavery education is almost the only thing in him to be lamented. That education is still in his way. It was emphatically so in the early stages of the war. It entangled him with the Border Slave States, when he should have been free with the Free States. Nevertheless, I take pleasure in acknowledging both his ability and honesty; and this I do notwithstanding I did not vote for him and that I never voted for his party. Some of the richest and sublimest comments on the Declaration of Independence which I have ever read, are from his pen. His letter to the officers of the Albany Democratic Convention, is a monument of his vigorous common-sense, of his clear and convincing logic, of his reasonableness and moderation, of his candor and frankness. On the whole, Washington always excepted, we have had no President who is to be more esteemed and beloved than Abraham Lincoln.

I said that not to stand by the Government is not to stand by the country. Every man who in time of war busies himself in slandering the Government and weakening the public confidence in it, is among the meanest and worst enemies of the country. How base and pernicious the slander that the Government is no longer prosecuting the war to save the country! A State Convention in Pennsylvania — and that too at the very time when the State was invaded and her capital threatened — improved upon this slander by deliberately resolving that the Government *avows* and *proclaims* that the saving of the country is no longer its object in the war. What wonder that there should be mobs against drafting soldiers when there are such incitements to such mobs!—when there is so much industry and so much art to persuade the people that the drafted soldiers are to be used, not for the one legitimate purpose, but for some sinister or party purpose! These mobs, though they fill us with sorrow, do nevertheless not surprise us. For we see them to be the natural and almost necessary fruit of those incessant declarations by unprincipled politicians that the Government has turned away from the object of saving the country, and is now calling for men and money wherewith to promote other and odious objects. Upon these knavish and lying politicians rest the blame and the blood of all these mobs.

In the second place, we are to insist on the immediate and unconditional submission of the rebels. Nothing short of this would suffice for their humiliation and their good. Moreover, nothing short of this would save our Government and our country from being deeply and indelibly disgraced—ay, totally wrecked and ruined. Therefore there must be no armistice, no terms. To bargain with them; to give them time; to make concessions to them; to purchase peace from them; to make any peace with them, whilst as yet they have arms in their hands, would be to leave them with even a more incorrigible spirit than they now have, and it would also be to leave ourselves without a nation. That which would be left to us would be but a nominal nation—and it would be liable to be broken up in a twelvemonth. What is more, neither the world, nor we ourselves, could ever have any respect for it. A nation that is *compelled* to yield to traitors may be respected by both other nations and itself. But a nation which has power to overwhelm the traitors, and yet is too corrupt or cowardly to wield it, must be, ever after, a stench both in its own and in others' nostrils. In the light of what I have just said it is not too much to add that whilst Americans who counsel peace on any lower terms than the absolute submission of the rebels are traitors, those speakers and writers in foreign lands who do likewise are hypocrites, because they well know that what they counsel for our nation they would, were it counseled for their own, promptly and indignantly reject.

In the third place, we must not be speculating on what is to be done with the rebels after they shall be conquered. Such speculation is wholly unseasonable and it but tends to divide us. Whilst as yet the rebels are unconquered, we can not afford to be divided. The needless, foolish, guilty, and exceedingly hurtful differences among us are what alone make our conquest of the rebels uncertain. When we shall have conquered them, then we can talk to our heart's content of what should be done with them and their possessions. Besides, we know not now in what mood they will be then; and therefore we know not now what it will be proper for them to receive at our hands. If they shall be impenitent and defiant, we shall need to impose very careful restrictions upon them; but if penitent and humble, then we can risk being trustful and generous toward them. And then, too, notwithstanding their enormous crimes against their country—against earth and heaven—we shall gladly look upon our sorrowful Southern brethren as our brethren still.

In the fourth place, we must insist that other nations shall let us alone. Ours is a family quarrel, and none but the family can be allowed to meddle with it. We can tolerate neither intervention

nor mediation. We shall repel both. Mediation, proffered in
however friendly a spirit, we shall regard as impertinence; and
intervention, although bloodless and unarmed at the beginning, we
shall from the beginning construe into war. And here let me add,
that whilst we very gratefully acknowledge the able advocacy of
our cause by many distinguished men of Europe, and no less gratefully the true, intelligent, and generous sympathy with it of the
masses of Europe; and that whilst we would not discourage our
citizens from going abroad to plead that cause; we, nevertheless,
are entirely convinced that the work to be done for our country
is to be done *in it*—to be done by earnest appeals from Americans
to Americans, and by hard blows from a loyal upon a disloyal
army.

Let us now pass on to consider what should be the character of
our opposition to the rebellion. I said that the rebels must be
unconditional in their submission. I add that our opposition to
the rebels must also be unconditional. The surrender of ourselves to our high and holy cause must be absolute. We must
stipulate for nothing. We must reserve nothing in behalf of our
Democratic, or Republican, or Abolition, or Temperance, or any
other party—nothing in behalf of any individual interests. Nay,
we must make no conditions in behalf of either the Constitution
or the country. We have now but one work. The putting down
of the rebellion is the supreme duty which America owes to herself, to mankind, and to God Is it said that recent events have
given us another work to to? the work of putting down and
keeping down mobs? I answer that these mobs are nothing
more nor nothing less than Northern branches and Northern
outbreaks of the Southern rebellion, and that the rebellion
ended, the mobs will also be ended. This, by the way, being
the true character of these mobs, the Federal war power is as
clearly bound to lay its restraining hand on those who get them
up as on any other parties to the rebellion. It should spare no
traitorous press, because of its great influence, and no traitorous
politician, because of his high office, when it is clear that they
have been at work to generate the passions and prejudices, the
treason and anarchy which have resulted in disturbances, so
frightfully marked, in some instances, by fire and blood.

These mobs, by the way, aside from their destruction of innocent and precious life, are not to be regretted. Nay, they are to
be rejoiced in, because they reveal so certainly and so fully the ani-
mus of the leaders of this " Northern Peace Party," and therefore
serve to put us more upon our guard against these desperate leaders. I am not at all surprised at hearing that many an honest
man, who had sympathized with this party, is so far enlightened
by these mobs as to turn away from it forever.

The motto of every man among us should be: " Down with
the Rebellion at whatever cost!" It must go down, even though
Constitution and country go down with it. If the rebellion
is to live and triumph, then let all else, however dear, die.

Not Constitution nor country, not our farms nor our merchandise, not our families nor our own lives, could be any longer of value to us. Are there Republicans who, in this trial hour of integrity, are intent on keeping their party in power? then are they false to their country. In time of peace let there be parties to represent the different views in regard to the proper character and conduct of the Government. But in time of war to cling to party is treason to the country. For then the great question is, no longer as in time of peace, how the Government shall be shaped and administered, but the infinitely greater one—whether we shall have a country to govern. Are there Democrats who, at such a time, are intent on getting their party into power? False to their country are they also. Is it their plea that they are talking for the Constitution? I answer, that their talk should be against the rebels. This talking for the Constitution, whilst not talking against the rebels, is but hypocrisy. Are there Abolitionists who say that they can not help put down the rebellion unless the Government will pledge itself to put down slavery? Let me say, that with such one-idea men I have no sympathy. Like the sham Republicans and sham Democrats I have referred to, they are but workers for the rebels. To all who feel this unseasonable and treasonable solicitude for party, let me say that the true doctrine is: "Come what will of it to the Republican, or Democratic, or Abolition, or any other party—though they all go to flinders and be reduced to a heap of ruins—the Rebellion, nevertheless, shall be put down!" Moreover, notwithstanding our differences in other relations and other respects, we are all to be brothers and close fellow-laborers in the work of putting down the Rebellion. The laborers in this work we are not to know as Democrats, or Republicans, or Abolitionists, or Temperance men, but only as anti-rebellion men. During the greater part of my life I have tried to do something against slavery and drunkenness. But in this great battle against the Southern rebels and their Northern allies, whose success would, in its results, be the entire overthrow of free Government, not only here and in Mexico, but wherever it exists, I am ready to fight alongside of all who will fight alongside of me: with, if you please, the biggest drunkard on the one side and the biggest pro-slavery man on the other. Whilst I am against all who are for the rebels, I am for all who are against them. Until the Rebellion is crushed we should know but two parties: the one made up of those who, in standing by and strengthening the Government, prove themselves to be the friends of the country; and the other made up of those who, in assailing and weakening the Government, prove themselves to be the enemies of the country. Are there, I repeat, Abolitionists who, in such a time as this, stand back and refuse to join in putting down the Rebellion save on the condition that slavery also shall be put down? If there are, then are they also among those who embarrass the Government, and then are they also to be numbered with the enemies of the country. If there are such

Abolitionists, I am persuaded they are few. But whether they are few or many, let me say that it is very little to their credit to let the crime of slavery fill the whole field of their vision and blind them to the far greater and more comprehensive crime of the rebellion. Will they reply, that the rebellion is but slavery — slavery in arms? Then upon their own ground they should be helping to put it down, since the putting of it down would be the putting down of slavery also.

I referred to Mexico. If our rebellion shall succeed, her fate is sealed. If it should fail, then it may even be that Napoleon's is sealed. I say not that our Government would be disposed to meddle with him. But I do say that our people would be. Tens of thousands of our disbanded troops would hasten to Mexico to make common cause with their outraged republican brethren. I add, that whilst despots everywhere would exult in the triumph of our rebellion, despots everywhere will tremble at its overthrow.

Some of my hearers may think, because I said we must make no conditions in its behalf, that I am not suited with the Constitution. I am entirely suited with it. I have always opposed changes in it, and probably always shall. No Democrat even has spoken or written so much for it *just as it is* as I have. Let not a word in it be altered. It is exactly what we want of a Constitution, both in peace and, war. Governor Seymour says, in his Fourth of July speech that the Government has suspended it. If it has, it has done very wrong. I do not see that it has in even the slightest degree. But there are some things which the Governor and I see with very different eyes. For instance, the Governor and the men of his school see that the blame of the war rests chiefly upon the North. On the other hand, I see that every particle of it rests on the South. They say that our talking and legislating against slavery annoyed the South; and we, in turn, say that her talking and legislating for it annoyed the North. But we deny that the annoyance did in either case justify war. As to the talking — it must be remembered that our Southern and Northern fathers agreed upon a Government, which tolerates talk—talk even against good things—against things which, if that be possible, are better than even slavery. So the South should not make war upon us because we talk against her slavery; and we should not make war upon her because she stigmatizes our noble farmers and noble mechanics as "the mudsills of society." Then, as to the legislation, it must be remembered that whilst we were willing to have the constitutionality of ours passed upon by the Supreme Court of the United States, she threatened to murder and actually drove from her the honorable men whom we deputed to visit her for the purpose of getting her consent to such a testing of her pro-slavery legislation. Truly, truly do I pity the man who is so perverted as to divide the blame of this war between the North and the South. The North is not only mainly but entirely innocent of it.

I eulogized the Constitution. Let not the eulogy be construed into my overrating of a Constitution. I frankly say that if I thought that our Constitution stood at all in the way of our most effective prosecution of the war, I should rejoice to have it swept out of the way. The country is more than the Constitution. I would not exchange one of her majestic mountains or rivers for all the Constitutions you could pile up between earth and heaven. God made the country. But man made the Constitution. The loss of the country would be irreparable. But if the Constitution is lost, we will rely upon his inspirations of the human mind for another.

I spoke disparagingly of one-idea men. There is a sense in which I wish that all of us were one-idea men. I would that all of us might be one-idea men until the Rebellion is put down. To put it down—this, this is the one idea of which I would have every man possessed to the exclusion of every rival idea. For the sake of no other idea would I have conditions made with this paramount idea. Were we all such one-idea men, the North would triumph speedily—and so grandly too as to win the admiration and esteem even of the South. And then would the North and the South again become a nation — not, as before, an inharmonious and short-lived one, but a nation at peace with itself, at peace with every other nation, and therefore a permanent nation. God grant us this glorious and blessed future! And he will grant it, if we are so manly and patriotic, so wise and just, as to postpone every other claim to that of our country and every other duty to that of putting down the Rebellion.

Let us now take up the Conscription Law. Some say that it is unconstitutional. I can not see any thing unconstitutional in it— though perhaps I could were I a lawyer. Some go so far as to deny that the Constitution gives Congress the right to compel persons to defend the country. All I can say is, that if it did not give the right, it should not have empowered Congress to declare war and raise and support armies. For thus to have empowered it was in that case but to mock it. It was only to seem to give much whilst really giving nothing.

For one, I do not look into the Constitution for proof that the National Legislature has the right to compel persons to fight the battles of the country. It is enough for me to know that this vital right inheres in a National Legislature—that the supreme power of a nation necessarily has it—and that a Constitution which should deny or in the slightest degree restrict it, would be fit only to be thrown away. For the credit of the Constitution, I am happy that it recognizes and asserts the right. But the Constitution does not create it. My refusal to look into the Constitution for the origination of this right rests on the same principle as that by which I am withheld from looking into the Bible for the origination of the parent's right to take care of his children. It is, I admit, one of the merits of this best of books that it recognizes the right and enjoins its exercise. But the right is older than the Bible. It dates as far back as the time of the first parent. It is an inherently parental as the other is an inherently national right.

It is also said that the Conscription Law favors the rich, and oppresses the poor. The National and State militia laws do so ; but the Conscription Law spares the poor and spares not the rich. Members of Congress, Postmasters, and a score of other classes, making in all no very small share of the men, are, under those laws, exempted from military service ; whilst under the Conscription Law none but poor men are exempted, save only the Vice-President, the Heads of Departments, the United States Judges, and the Governors of the States. And now mark how numerous must be the several classes of the exempted poor.

1st. The only son of the widow dependent on his labor.

2d. The only son of aged or infirm parents dependent on his labor.

3d. One of the two or more sons of such parents.

4th. The only brother of orphan children not twelve years old dependent on his labor.

5th. The father of motherless children under twelve years of age dependent on his labor.

6th. Where there are a father and sons in the family, and two of them are in the army and in humble positions in it, the residue not exceeding two are exempt.

Now, was there ever a law less sparing of the rich and more tender to the poor ? And yet this law, so exceedingly honorable to the heads and hearts of its makers, is denounced as oppressive and cruel by demagogues who, to get themselves into power, would destroy the popular confidence in the Government and destroy the country also.

But, it is held, that the commutation or three hundred dollar clause is oppressive to the poor. It is, on the contrary, merciful to the poor. But for it the price of a substitute might run up to three or four times three hundred dollars—a price which a poor man would scarcely ever be enabled to pay. The three hundred dollars, however, many a poor man can, with the help of friends, be able to raise. But why not, it may be asked, have favored the poor by making the maximum no more than fifty or a hundred dollars ? This, instead of favoring, would have but oppressed the poor. For the Government, not being able to procure substitutes at the rate of fifty or a hundred dollars, would have been compelled to repeat its drafts. And thus tens of thousands of poor men who had paid their fifty or a hundred dollars in order to keep out of the army would after all be obliged to enter it.

Alas ! this clamor against the unconstitutionality of the Con-scription Law ! How sadly it betrays the prevailing lack of patriotism ! Had there been no unpatriotic person amongst us, there would have been not only nothing of this clamor, but not so much as one inquiry into the constitutionality of the law. The commonness of this inquiry indicates how commonly the love of country must be very weak in the American bosom. Why is it so weak? Some say it is because of our characteristic or Yankee greed of gain; and some say it is because of our long-continued and soul-shriveling practice of persecuting and outraging an unfortunate race. Some ascribe it to one thing and some to another. But whatever the cause, the effect is obvious.

Oh! how base must they have become who, when rebels are at the throat of their nation, can hie themselves to the Constitution to see how little it will let them off with doing against those rebels—how little with doing for the life of that nation! Our noble Constitution should be used to nourish our patriotism; but alas! it is perverted to kill it!

I have noticed the action of the authorities of several of the cities of our State, in regard to the Conscription Law. In some of them this action is very bad. The sole object of the law is to raise an additional force for completing the destruction of the Rebellion. Now, the city of New-York and some other cities would take advantage of its humane feature of commutation to defeat this sole object of the law. For they would take advantage of it to buy off the mass of their drafted citizens. This wholesale buying violates to the last degree the spirit of the law; deprives the country of the benefit of the legitimate and intended effect of the law; and saves the Rebellion from being crushed by the faithful and fair carrying out of the law. If one city may resort to this wholesale buying, so may every other; so may every county, and so may every State; and so may the Conscription Law be rendered unavailing.

I admit the duty of the wealthy to avail themselves of this commutation clause to save, here and there, from going to the war the man to whom it would be a peculiar hardship to go. I also admit that every city, disposed to do so, can very properly vote the three hundred dollars to every drafted man who serves or to his substitute. I care not how much the cities help the soldiers. The more the better. I am glad that Oswego voted ten thousand dollars two years ago, and five thousand last spring to the families of her soldiers. Let her vote hereafter as much as she pleases to the soldiers and their families. I will pay cheerfully what share of the tax shall fall on my property in the city; and more cheerfully would I take part in voluntary contributions.

I have sometimes heard the remark that neither the rich nor the poor should be allowed to procure substitutes. The remark is both ill-natured and foolish. Among the drafted will be both rich and poor men, who ought to be spared from going to the war. I am not sorry that so many rich men have gone to the war. Nevertheless, let as many rich men as will remain at home to continue to give employment to the poor in manufactories and elsewhere, and to maintain a business and a prosperity which can be heavily taxed to meet the expenses of the war. Men of property should be heavily taxed to this end; and my only objection to the

Income Tax, is that it is not more than half large enough. It should be six and ten instead of three and five per cent.

But I must close. How unreasonable, how unpatriotic, how wicked to murmur at this draft! The South, to serve her bad cause, is, at this moment, responding to the call for absolutely all her able-bodied white males between the ages of eighteen and forty-five; whilst the call to serve our best of all causes is for not more than about one seventh or one eighth between those ages. And yet we murmur at the draft; and in a few localities there is a rabble so far under the sway of traitorous demagogues, as to resist it with force and arms. These demagogues, by the way, as silly as they are wicked, instead of seeing in this resistance only another argument with the Government for proceeding promptly, very promptly with the draft, flattered themselves that the Government would succumb to the mobs and abandon the draft; would surrender to anarchy instead of maintaining law.

Our people need to be loyally educated. When they are, they will be eager to serve their imperiled and beloved country in any way, however expensive or hazardous. I rejoice to see that in many parts of the country the draft is met in a cheerful and patriotic spirit. May this spirit soon obtain everywhere

The love of country—the love of country—that is what we lack. Would that we had somewhat of that love of country which Robert Emmet felt for his dear Ireland; somewhat of that love of country which awakens the sublime utterances of Kossuth for his dear Hungary; somewhat of that love of country which stirs the great soul of Garibaldi, as he contemplates his still, but not-ever-to-be, disunited Italy; somewhat of that love of country which arms her young men, ay and her young maidens too, to battle for their down-trodden and dear Poland! Let us have somewhat of such love — and then when our bleeding country makes her call upon us, we shall not pause to inquire whether it is couched in Constitutional words; but we shall hasten to obey it, simply because it is our country that makes it, and our country that needs our obedience.

SPEECH AT YOUNG MEN'S MASS CONVENTION,

IN

SYRACUSE, SEPTEMBER 3d, 1863.

It was my good fortune to be in the Convention when the President's admirable and unanswerable letter was read—was so well read—so dramatically and effectively read. I felt at the close of it, that we could afford to adjourn the Convention at that moment *sine die*. I felt that we would be warranted in returning to our homes and telling our neighbors that we had been in the best Convention we had ever been in ; and that the President's letter was of itself a full feast for the patriotic heart. But the Convention desired speaking also. They have had from Lieut.-Governor Noble a speech that kindled their patriotism to the highest pitch, and that convulsed them with its abounding wit. The man who follows him with a plain speech is at no little disadvantage. Nevertheless, it is wholesome to have a little plain fare mixed up with our rich fare. There is another embarrassment that I am under. I am so delighted with the President's letter that I do not know that I shall be able to compose myself to make a sober speech; and I should be sorry to have my speech marked with the intoxication of joy.

We read that on a certain occasion Moses stood and said : "Who is on the Lord's side? let him come unto me." He did not ask : " Who is of the tribe of Judah or Benjamin, or who is of any other tribe—who is of this party or that—who has these views or those?" His simple and sole inquiry was : " Who is on the Lord's side?"

And so when traitors have risen up to destroy our nation, there is but one question for us to put. It is: "Who is on the side of the country?" By the way, none who at such a time do not hasten to the side of their country, can give much evidence of being on the Lord's side.

Why is it, gentlemen, that I am here? It is thirty-five years this year since I have taken part in a Democratic, or a Whig, or a Republican meeting; and I never in my life was in a Native American meeting. If only because one of my grand-parents was born in Ireland, it would be ungracious in me to countenance a

meeting which is a meeting against the foreign-born. I am here,
gentlemen, because I heard you call: "Who is on the side of the
country?" Once some of you were members of the Democratic
party; and your call then was: "Who is on the side of the Democratic party?" Once some of you were of the Republican
party; and your call then was: "Who is on the side of the Republican party?" For one I did not listen to either call. I was
too much interested in other things to be much interested in party
politics. But now when your call is, "Who is on the side of the
country?"—now, when I see you have sunk party in patriotism
and are making more account of country than of the sum total of
all other earthly interests—now, I am quick to hear you and glad
to come to you. Now, I am with you "arm and soul." Now my
lot is cast in with yours. And now I exclaim from the heart:
"*Una spes unaque salus ambobus erit.*"

I commend you, gentlemen, for your giving up of party. I say
not that political party should never be. On the contrary, I admit that honest and wide differences of opinion in regard to the
proper character and conduct of Government, may render party
justifiable, if not indeed necessary, in time of peace. But in time of
war, when the question is whether there will be a Government left
us to differ about—nay, whether there will be so much as a country
left us to govern—then clearly all should give up party, and join
hands to save the country. The Republican party has done well
to disband. Alas! that the Democratic party did not also disband!

Party in time of war is the greatest of all evils and the heaviest
of all curses. I am so old as to remember the war of 1812-15;
and to remember how party then divided the country and her
councils; and how party interests, and the Hartford Convention, and other party measures brought the country to the brink of
ruin. Of course we all remember how quick was party in our
present war to raise its snaky, hissing, hated head. No sooner
had the President called for the seventy-five thousand men to save
the country from the traitors who were threatening to march upon
it, than party sent up the cry that the war was unconstitutional.
While patriotism was calling out earnestly to save the country,
party was calling out hypocritically to save the Constitution. The
really humane would save the drowning man. The pretendedly
humane are very solicitous to save his hat. The conventional and
fashion-bound Englishman would not rescue the drowning man,
because he had not been introduced to him. The Englishman's
order of doing things was, first to be introduced to the man and
afterward to save him. With no less absurdity do these demagogues put the saving of the Constitution before the saving of the
country. For a quarter of a century I have spoken and written
abundantly for that instrument—for that instrument just as it is—
line for line and letter for letter. But now, when my country is
in such fearful peril, my absorbing concern is to save her. I would
save her with the Constitution if I could; but with or without the

Constitution I would save her. The country is more than the Constitution. Much do I love the Constitution; but I love my country infinitely more. Let me, however, here say, that I know not that the Government has claimed any unconstitutional power in the prosecution of this war. It certainly did not need to. The Constitution gives all needed power for the most effective prosecution of the war.

It was the Democratic party that was appealed to (and alas so successful!) by this cry to save the Constitution. I am not saying that this party was less worthy than the Republican party. Had the Democratic party been in power when the war broke out, it would, I trust, have conducted the war loyally and vigorously, and successfully; and the Republican party, had it in that case kept up its organization, would, I fear, have proved as factious and disloyal as the Democratic party has proved itself. I care not what party it is—Republican or Democratic—if it keeps up its organization in time of war, it will soon show that it sets party above the country. This will be emphatically true if it is a party against those who are carrying on the war. Nothing has gone further to show the selfishness, baseness, and treasonableness of the Democratic party than its incessant claim through this war, that the war can never be brought to a successful close but by the Democratic party. How we are disgraced in the eyes of Europe by this declaration, that our country can be saved not by the country, but by party! And how much encouragement it has ministered to the rebels!

But some of you may be disposed to remind me that the old Democratic party kept up its organization during the last war. It did, and the blame of it was due quite as much to the Federal party as to the Democratic. The keeping up of the Federal organization provoked the keeping up of the Democratic. The truth is, that neither of these parties was what it should be. The Democratic party favored France and the Federal party favored England. The Democratic party followed the fortunes of the elder Napoleon, and the Federal party was not yet weaned from its degrading partiality for England. Not until after our last war with England were our political parties above serving foreign powers.

Let us glance at some of the evils that have sprung from the maintenance of party organization during this war.

First, during the whole war, party has been calling on the government to compromise with the rebels and patch up a peace with them. And this, too, notwithstanding the rebels have incessantly replied that they would consent to no peace with us but on the condition of their being allowed to dismember the nation and become entirely independent of us. Party has even gone so far as to propose that we come under the Southern or Montgomery Constitution. But even at this point she has spurned us. On no terms, however advantageous to herself or humiliating to us, would she consent to live with us. The degrading attitude toward her, during this war, of many of our Northern politicians has very much increased her contempt of us. She always despised us for our truckling to her.

And what if the rebels were willing to make peace with us, could we consent to make peace with them, whilst as yet they have arms in their hands, without covering our nation with infamy, and sinking it in ruin? Certainly not. We are not now to make peace with them; but we are to insist on their unconditional submission; and we are to keep on pursuing and pressing and punishing them until we have brought them to it. Unconditional must be our opposition to the rebels, and unconditional must be their submission to us. We are to carry on the war, stipulating for nothing in behalf of our Democratic, or Republican, or Abolition party, or tariffs, or aught else; and they are to lay down their arms, stipulating for nothing in behalf of their houses, or lands, or slaves, or free trade, or aught else.

The question is often put whether we would consent to receive back a Rebel State. Certainly we would. On what conditions? it is asked. On the condition of her unconditional surrender. But on what conditions beyond that? it is asked. We rejoin that we have not one word to say, nay, hardly one thought to think about further conditions until the first one has been complied with and she has surrendered absolutely. When our child has revolted against our parental authority, he is first to submit to it ere he is entitled to even the least intimations of what will be our subsequent treatment of him. It will be time enough after her submission to say, and perhaps time enough even to think, what we shall do with her after her submission. To take up that question now is but to multiply divisions among ourselves, and to make it uncertain whether we shall be able to compel her submission. The rebels, guilty, without the least provocation, of attempting to destroy our nation, are surely entitled to know nothing of what we shall do with them after we have conquered them. They must resign themselves to our measure of justice, generosity, and forgiveness; and I trust, that they will not find us greatly lacking in these virtues. For one I have never taken pleasure in this talk about banishing, imprisoning and hanging the rebels. Our Southern brethren some of them are very wicked, and more of them deeply deluded. But they are our brethren still; and I hope that should we succeed in conquering them, we shall be disposed to make every concession to them which is compatible with their safety and ours, their welfare and ours.

I notice that the Democratic leaders are very desirous to save Slavery. I admit that we should be very desirous to save every very good thing; and I am not denying that Slavery is a very good thing. But these leaders go further and insist that in the putting down of the Rebellion, Slavery shall be saved. In this, however, they are as wrong as are those abolitionists who insist that the putting down of the Rebellion shall be conditioned on the putting down of Slavery. But the true doctrine on this point is that the Rebellion shall go down, whether Slavery shall or shall

not go down with it. Our one common work is to put down the
Rebellion : and no part of that one common work is to put up or
to put down Slavery. I readily admit that a people may suffer
wrongs so deep as to justify them in breaking up their national
relations. But the only wrong we ever did the South was, to in-
dulge her and let her have her own way. I confess that we did
in this wise contribute largely to spoil her. This is our only offense against her.

I proceed in my mention of some of the evils which have grown
out of the maintenance of party during this war. From the first,
party has been so unpatriotic and insane as to object to our accepting the help of the negro. Whenever it has been proposed to let
him fight for us, party, playing upon the popular prejudice against
the negro, has objected to turning the war into a war for the
negro. I admit that it is not a war for the negro, and that it is
not a war for the abolition of Slavery. I admit that it is a war
for nothing else than to put down a base, brutal, abominable,
causeless, accursed Rebellion. But how disingenuous, how wicked, how absurd to say that letting the negro fight for us is turning
the war into a war for the negro! As well might it be said that
letting the Indians fight for us is turning it into a war for the
Indians. I have seen within a few days that the Kansas Indians
offer us their assistance in punishing the plundering and murderous invaders of Kansas. Shall we decline this assistance for fear
that accepting it will give the Democrats another occasion for
charging us with perverting the war?

Common-sense teaches us that we should get the negro to help
us if we can; and the Indian also if we can ; and the devil himself
if we can. I would that we could succeed in getting our harness
upon his back and in making him work for us. It would by the
way, be doing a great favor to the old rascal to make him serve a
good cause once in his life. To serve so good a cause as ours
would improve even so bad a character as the devil's.

And here let me say that had the Government brought negroes
into the Army as fast as it should, (and it should have brought
them in as fast as it could,) there would have been no need of this
draft, which is so trying to the North. Very trying it is, if only
because our innumerable departments of industry, which are all so
especially active at this time, can not well spare any laborers.
Why did not the Government take the black man who wanted to
fight for us, and spare the white man who preferred to remain in
his family and business ? I blame the Government at this point.
It is true that I blame the Democratic party for keeping up its
clamor against using the black man, and for thus making the Government afraid to use him. But I blame the Government also for
allowing itself to be frightened out of its duty. I admit that the
Government has shown itself strong at many points. But there is
one point where it has been wont to show itself weak. I refer
to its excessive desire to propitiate the Democratic party and

4

avoid its censure. Its true policy was to study to please its friends
rather than to avoid displeasing its enemies. Nevertheless, I like
the government. It is an honest, patriotic, and able government.
I say this though I did not vote for it, and though I never voted
the Republican ticket. I say it, too, though I had the same cause
for rebelling against the government which the South had. She
rebelled because Lincoln was elected. But Lincoln was no more
my candidate than he was hers. If she might rebel simply because an election went against her, so might I when one went
against me. There is this difference between the South and myself; I stand by the country, however an election may go; and
she trys to destroy it if an election does not go to suit her. I add
here in connection with what I said a little way back, that it is
not for Democrats to denounce the draft. Their party was opposed to letting negroes come into the army, and so white men
had to be drafted into it. It is the policy of his own party that
compels the drafted Democrat to serve in the place of the negro.
The negro stood ready to serve in the place of the white man;
but the Democratic party would not consent to it.

I go on to say that the late mobs are amongst the sad fruits of
keeping up party in time of war. These mobs were an open join-
ing of Northern traitors with Southern traitors. Shouts for the
Southern traitors were often heard in them. None but enemies of
the Government and friends of the rebels were in them. In a
word, none but Democrats. Can, the Democratic party live under
so damning a fact? I think not. Had it disbanded when the
war broke out, there would have been none of these mobs to disgrace and damn it. There would then have been no demagogues
to get them up; no Vallandighams and Woods to talk and write
treason; and no newspapers to print it, and urge the Governor
Seymours to practice it.

I need mention no more of the workings and fruits of this maintenance of party in time of war. Said I not well that such maintenance is the greatest of all perils and curses? As soon as war
begins party should be dropped. The demagogue, who after that
keeps on juggling with party names and party words, is the most
dangerous enemy of his country. For in this wise he is able to
lead against his country in time of war the many who, with comparative harmlessness, had been accustomed to follow him in time
of peace. No men at the South—not even the Davis's and Stephens's—are so dangerous to us as these Northern demagogues who
in time of war slander and embarrass the Government; poison and
pervert the public mind; get up mobs; and succeed in electing to
office men who are in sympathy with the South. Our motto should
be, "No party in war."

Again, I say that our common work now is to put down the Rebellion. Come what will of the putting of it down to the Democratic or Republican or Abolition party, it must be put down.
Come what will of it to Slavery or Anti-Slavery, it must be put
down. Slavery may be *incidentally* helped or harmed by it. But -

neither the helping nor harming of it is an *object* of this one common work.

By all, then, that is precious in our country, which they are so fearfully imperiling by continuing in the Democratic party, would I exhort the honest masses of that party to quit it. And I would have them join no other until the Rebellion is crushed. I do not exhort them to quit it because it is the Democratic party, but simply because it keeps up its organization in time of war. When peace shall return to bless our blood-soaked land, they can again, if they please, become members of the Democratic party. I say nothing against either a Democratic or a Republican party, only that neither should be kept up in time of war.

By all, too, that is precious in a good name—a good name to be enjoyed by ourselves and to be transmitted to our children—would I exhort the honest masses of the Democratic party to quit it. The boldest and most unprincipled portion of its leaders will stamp its character; and necessarily, therefore, it will be a very black one—so black as to reflect not a little disgrace upon every man who belongs to the party. Why will the memory of the Vallandighams and Woods rot—or if it live, live but to be loathed? Because they were guilty of the crime, ay, of the treason, of clinging to party in war, and of using party against their country. And why will the Dickinsons and Butlers be ever bright and beautiful upon the page of history? Because when war came they gave up party for country.

By all, too, that is mortifying in a signal and utter failure, would I exhort the honest masses of the Democratic party to quit it. The Rebellion will go down. It will go down into the lowest depths of infamy, destruction, and despair. And the Democratic party, because its leaders have identified it with the Rebellion, will go down with the Rebellion. Yes, it will go down as disgraced, as deep and as dead as the Rebellion. The Federal party had to die immediately after our last war with England, because it had placed itself in the way of our Government's prosecution of that war. The Democratic party is opposing the Government's putting down of the guiltiest enemies a nation ever had; and therefore the Democratic party must also die.

Let me, in closing, say, that not only traitorous Democrats will find their damnation in this war; but that every other man, be he Republican or Abolitionist, will find it, if he traitorously refuses to identify himself with the endeavors of our honest and earnest Government, and of our brave and immortalized army and navy to put down this infernal Rebellion. No one of them all—if, indeed, any moral sensibility can survive in him—but will feel, under the outpourings upon him of the world's scorn and disgust, that it were better for him had he never been born.

THE REBELLION.

SPEECH IN MONTREAL, DEC. 19TH, 1863.

I CHOSE this time for visiting Montreal because I saw in the newspapers that a case involving the reputation of one of my old and dear friends (Hon. J. R. Giddings) was to be tried in your courts at this time. Being in your city, I was not only willing but glad to consent to make a speech on the state of my country.

I love Canada. My own mother was born on the banks of your Sorel. It has ever been my desire that my country and yours should be peaceable and pleasant neighbors. I was a member of the American Congress when, nine years ago, it sanctioned the Reciprocity Treaty between us. Other members' may have worked for that sanction more influentially and efficiently, but none worked harder for it than I did. It is extensively believed in my country that the treaty is more advantageous to you than to us; and I notice a present movement in Congress for discontinuing it. I hope that it and every other movement to this end may fail. I love the treaty. I love it, because it tends to promote friendly intercourse and to multiply ties between us. This is, in my judgment, far more important than to make money out of it. I am, myself, in favor of an absolutely free trade. I would not have a custom-house on the earth. I believe that the great and good Father of us all would have his children left free to buy and sell in all the markets. I would, of course, have the exchanges between nations include merchandise and manufactures. But if there are nations that refuse to include them, I, nevertheless, would not have my nation refuse to exchange natural productions with such nations.

My country is sorely afflicted. A Rebellion, the most gigantic and also the most guilty the world ever saw, has broken out against her. Nevertheless, all Canadians do not sympathize with her. I do not infer this from the fact that persons within her borders have recently sought to make Canada a base of military operations against us. These persons, I doubt not, were nearly all refugees from my own country. I am sure the Canadians did not countenance the crime. Nor did their Government. Nay, I am informed that it was some one in their Government (thanks to that some one!) who informed Lord Lyons of the plot. Thanks to Lord Lyons also, who, as the story runs, left his bed at midnight to inform my Government of it! No, it is not from this that I infer the lack of Canadian sympathy. It is from other things, and especially from the spirit of many of the Canadian newspapers. There are Canadian newspapers, and some of them are in this city, that speak rightly of our Rebellion. I read the *Toronto Globe:* and I would that all your newspapers spoke of the Rebellion in the spirit in which that able and excellent newspaper speaks of it.

I said that I love Canada. I add that I love Great Britain also. Toward her as well as toward Canada I stand in filial relations. For my mother's mother was born in green Ireland: and if having a Livingston for a grandfather makes a Scotchman, then am I a Scotchman also. But more than this, all men of my advanced age, whose childhood's language was the English, are more or less educated by Great Britain. Our manners, habits, characters come in no small degree from the moulding influences of her statesmen, historians, poets, and novelists.

I referred to the lack in Canada of sympathy with my distressed country. There is the like lack in Great Britain also. I do not infer it from her acknowledgment of belligerent rights in the rebels. I justify that acknowledgment: and my country should feel herself estopped from complaining of it by the fact that she found herself obliged to accord these rights to the rebels. The simple truth is, that the rebels were too numerous to be treated as pirates and outlaws. Just here however let me say that burning captured ships at sea is not among belligerent rights. If the rebels have no ports into which to take the captured vessel for adjudication, then so far they have no belligerent rights. Nor do I infer this lack of British sympathy from the fact that British-built vessels have gone out from British ports to be used by the rebels in preying upon the commerce of my country. I am sure that the people of Great Britain do not approve this: and the British Government is giving honorable and satisfactory testimony that it also does not approve it. Moreover, not only the British conscience but the British interest is against it. For Great Britain to justify or to suffer this indirect war upon us would be to leave herself without cause of complaint when in turn we should treat her so. That we should be provoked to such retaliation is well-nigh certain. Nor do I argue this lack of sympathy in Great Britain from her treatment of us in the Trent affair—wrong as I think it to have been. A word about that treatment. I will, if you say so, admit that international law was on her side in that affair. I will, if you say so, admit that there was no impropriety, no indecency, no affectation in the firing up of her indignation at that in our one vessel the like of which we had suffered from many scores of her vessels. And I will too, if you say so, admit that her Government had the right to make no account of the certain knowledge it had seasonably come into possession of, that our Government had not indorsed the acts of Captain Wilkes. Never-

theless, after making all these admissions, I must still hold that in
the Trent affair your country did mine a great and a grievous wrong.
For without giving a moment's time for negotiation she virtually
declared war: loading her cannon and lighting the match, and
giving us but time to fall down upon our knees and beg her pardon. And all this too when we had upon our hands a most fearful
civil war. And all this too when she knew that Captain Wilkes
did not only not intend any wrong to British interests, but did
intend to preserve them all most carefully. And all this too when
she knew that Captain Wilkes's not taking the Trent into port for adjudication was because of his deep desire to save her and the interests
embarked in her from inconvenience and loss. But you will say
that Captain Wilkes insulted the British flag. To this I answer
that there is not the slightest evidence that he intended to. Nevertheless he did, will be your rejoiner. I know what is the British
spirit—the British jealousy—in regard to the British flag, and especially when it floats over a ship—for Britain is even more of a
water than land-fowl. I will not say aught in derogation or complaint of this spirit. But this much I will say—that on the same
wise and Christian principle that an individual should not return
an insult with a blow, a nation should not. England regards herself, and I will not say unjustly, as the foremost nation in Christian
civilization. But how sad that a nation thus advanced should be
ready to go to war for a point of honor! Perhaps you will say that
my own nation would do so. I fear she would. This, however, would
only show that my nation, like yours, has not yet risen into obedience to all the laws of Christ.

No, it is not from the things I have mentioned that I argue
Britain's lack of sympathy with my greatly afflicted country. I
argue it from the tone of a large share of the British press ; from
a class of speeches made in many British meetings and the responses to them ; and from the reports of many Americans, who,
in their visits to England, frequently encounter, in both high places
and low, expressions of very ill feeling toward my country.

I proceed to ask why it is that so many Britons on both sides
of the Atlantic sympathize with the rebels.

First. Is it, because of a jealousy of our vast and mighty Republic ? *It is*, said one of your intelligent citizens to me, as I sat in
the car by his side, the morning I entered your city: and this
gentleman justified the jealousy. But I hope he was wrong in as-
cribing this British sympathy to so unworthy a cause. We certainly ought to accord to every people their choice of government.
I am not myself for the "Monroe Doctrine" to the extent that
most of my countrymen are. If Mexico prefers a monarchical
government, I would let her have it. And I say this notwithstanding my life-long advocacy of the most ultra democratic
theories of government. I would leave Europe free to persuade
all republican America to adopt monarchy. On the other hand
America should be left free to attempt the conversion of monarchical Europe. But in neither case compulsion.

Second. Does this British sympathy for the rebels spring from faith in the doctrine of " Secession"? This doctrine grows out of the claim that the States, which compose the United States, are nations—are sovereignties—notwithstanding they have not sovereign power enough to coin a sixpence. How strange if they are indeed nations and sovereignties, that England has never found it out before! She, in common with all Europe, has gone on maintaining diplomatic relations with our one nation at Washington, instead of with a score or two of nations at Boston, New-York, Baltimore, New-Orleans, etc. Then if these States are all nations and sovereignties, our Constitution must surely show so important a fact. But it shows that the people of the United States (and by the way, not the *States* of the United States) made, not a plurality of Constitutions for a plurality of nations, but one Constitution for one nation. And how absurd is the doctrine that our one nation is the agent of a score or two of nations! An agent is held to be inferior to his principals, inasmuch as they appoint and commission him. But in this case the agent, if agent he be, is immensely superior to his principals :—for instead of their watching him and having power over him, he watches them and has power over them. For instance, he is to see to it that they maintain a republican form of government. And so, too, instead of his being governed by their laws, they are governed by his—and that too even when his are right in the face of theirs. And what is still more degrading to these claimed-to-be principals, they are required to swear allegiance to him instead of his being required to swear allegiance to them. How humiliating it must have been to his brethren's sheaves if they had actually to do obeisance to the boy Joseph's sheaf! And how humiliating it must have been to the sun and moon and eleven stars if they too had actually to make obeisance to him! But scarcely less humiliating to the numerous States in the United States is their submission to the one reputed nation of the United States, if they are all nations, and this one reputed nation is not a nation; or if, in other words, they are the principals and this but their agent. The doctrine of the right of our States to secede is simply ridiculous. That the people, in adopting the Constitution, voted by States was a convenience, which could not well be dispensed with. But it was a *necessity* also, inasmuch as in this wise only could the assent of the people of each State to that loss of State rights and State sovereignty, which the Constitution called for, be obtained.

Third. Was it because the Southern States were oppressed by a High Tariff, that Britons sympathized with them ? But the Morrill or High Tariff was not enacted until the March after the December in which the States began to secede. And, by the way, one justification for enacting it was that our Government would needs its avails in reducing those States. We never had a Tariff so welcome to the Southern States as that we had when the Rebellion begun. None of our previous tariffs made so great approaches to the policy of Free Trade. But no tariff, high or low, is an excuse for War.

Fourth. Was this British sympathy with the rebels caused by the growing disposition in my country, as indicated by the triumph of Freedom in Kansas, to keep Slavery out of the Territories? But there is nothing in the Constitution to forbid the growth of such a disposition: and I would hope that there is nothing in your hearts to forbid it.

Fifth. Was the election of Mr. Lincoln the cause of this sympathy? I confess that it was no small trial of Southern patience to have a man elected to the Presidency, who was opposed to letting Slavery go into the Territories. But the Constitution, which allowed the election of his Pro-Slavery predecessors, equally allowed his election. The North did not rebel because of the former: and the South should not have rebelled because of the latter. Submission to the will of the majority lies at the very foundation of the Government chosen and constructed by the American fathers.

Sixth. Was this sympathy because of the Northern talk and Northern legislation against Slavery? But free speech is expressly provided for in our Constitution: and hence the South had no more right to rebel when we denounced her system of slave-labor than we had when she was stigmatizing our noble farmers and mechanics as "mudsills" and "greasy fists." As to the legislation against Slavery, the North was always ready to have the Supreme Court of the United States pass upon its Constitutionality. There was legislation at the South in favor of Slavery, which the North believed to be unconstitutional. She began to send down Commissioners to the South to invite her to unite with them in measures for bringing such legislation under the review of that Court. But these Commissioners were threatened with murder and forcibly expelled.

Seventh. Finally, do Britons sympathize with the Rebellion because the Rebels saw that Slavery was unsafe in the old nation and under the old Constitution: that in order to maintain, extend, and perpetuate it, they must have a new nation with Slavery for its boasted corner-stone—a new nation whose Constitution would recognize property in man as fully and absolutely as it exists in brutes? Such a Constitution they already have; and such a nation they are trying to have. And here let me say, that to have such a Constitution and such a nation was their sole object in rebelling. As to the election of Lincoln, they were more glad of it than sorry for it, since it furnished them, for use among the ignorant and undesigning, with a pretext for the Rebellion. The Northern Anti-Slavery legislation was also, on the whole, welcome to them, since it too helped furnish them with this pretext. As to the Northern talk against Slavery, they of course knew that they could not get away from it by getting out of the nation. I need not add that the Tariff was not amongst their grievances—for it was already low, and had they remained in the nation they could have made it lower. I ask again, do Britons sympathize with the Rebellion because it originated in the motive of serving and advancing Slavery? But Britons are opposed to Slavery:—and how therefore can they regard with favor an undertaking to "lengthen the cords and strengthen the stakes" of Slavery?—an undertaking never before known—that is, to create a nation solely for the slaveholder?[*]

I have done with asking why Britons sympathize with the Rebellion. I hear of no worthy reason for it. There can be none. I will now pass on to mention two grounds on which your sympathy with my country is claimed, and on neither of which you are bound to sympathize with it.

First. There are writers and orators at the North, who ask the world to favor the cause of the North on the ground that she is prosecuting the war for the overthrow of Slavery. But she is not prosecuting it for that purpose. It is true that slavery has been much damaged by the war:—only incidentally, however. It is true that Slavery will lose its life in this war. The first gun discharged at Sumter shot death into Slavery. From that moment it has never been possible to save it. On the other hand, it is also true that the Government, in carrying on the war, has aimed neither to uphold nor overthrow Slavery. It has aimed simply to suppress the Rebellion and preserve the nation. This has been its only object: and whenever it has touched Slavery it has been but to subserve and secure this object.

I further admit that, whilst there are many persons (shame to them!) who would have the Government pervert the war into a war for upholding Slavery, there are on the other hand a few persons, chiefly Abolitionists of misguided zeal, who would have the Rebellion put down only on the condition that Slavery be put down with it. Some of them claim that they herein conform to God's policy. But I must believe that they misinterpret God. My own philosophy teaches, that God would have us put down every sin (and where is there a greater sin than this Rebellion?) unconditionally, uncalculatingly, uncompromisingly. My own philosophy teaches, that we are never to wait, not even an hour nor

[*]Alexander H. Stephens, the Vice-President of the Confederacy, and an eminently intellectual man, is good authority for saying, first, that the North gave the South no cause to rebel; secondly, that to serve and advance the interests of Slavery was the object of rebelling. In his speech of November fourteenth, 1860, in the Hall of the House of Representatives of Georgia, Mr. Stephens, who as yet opposed the Rebellion, said: "What right has the North assailed? What interest of the South has been invaded? What justice has been denied, or what claim founded in justice and right has been withheld? Can any of you to-day name one governmental act of wrong deliberately and purposely done by the government at Washington of which the South has a right to complain? I challenge the answer." Then in the month of March, 1861, and when, notwithstanding his earnest attempts to lay the storm, he found himself swept away by it, and made the second officer in the new nation, he declared in his speech in Savannah, that "the new Constitution had put at rest forever all the agitating questions relating to" Slavery; and that "our new Government is founded upon exactly the opposite ideas" of the old Government and "upon the great truth that Slavery is his (the negro's) natural and moral condition."

a moment, to put down a sin, in the hope that by waiting we shall
be able to drag down some other sin with it. The sins of earth
will go down quickest if we try to put down each as soon as we
can.

Second. Your sympathy with the cause of my country is also
claimed by Northern orators and writers on the ground that
whilst the Southern people are Pro-Slavery the Northern are
quite extensively Abolitionists. But you should not sympathize
with us on this ground, for it is a false one. It is true that the
North is immeasurably less Pro-Slavery than the South: and
that in the progress and through the teachings of this war, it is
constantly becoming less and less Pro-Slavery. But it is also
true that no large proportion of the people of the North are as
yet Abolitionist. Our evil inheritance of Slavery from England,
whilst corrupting to the very core the people of the South, corrupted very deeply the people of the North also. At the North
as well as at the South "Abolitionist" is still the most reproach-
ful, odious, and shunned of all names. Not only do the people
of the South, but very generally the people of the North also,
refuse to sit at table or in the house of worship by the side of
the black man. As an outcast Pariah, as an unclean leper, is the
black man as well at the North as at the South. Very extensively at the North is the Bible still held to be for Slavery.
Bishop Hopkins of your neighboring Vermont so holds: and
simply because he so holds, the Pro-Slavery party tried a few
days ago to make him one of the chaplains of Congress. The
wickedness of running to the blessed Bible for sanction of the
highest possible crime is still very common at the North. The
folly of trying to prove by a book that Slavery is right—a folly
no less than would be that of trying to prove by it that two and
two make five, or that a circle is a square—is still one of the
follies of the North. By the way, what could any book, however sacred, be worth, which teaches *that* to be right in which
there is not one element of right—nay, not one element but what
is utterly and infernally wrong? And the practice still obtains
at the North of according the Pro-Slavery construction to the
Constitution—to a Constitution which, whilst it contains not one
line nor one word for Slavery, expressly declares that: "No person
shall be deprived of life, liberty, or property without due process
of law." Yes, the people of the North do still very generally accept
the Pro-Slavery interpretation of the Constitution. And they go
so far as to reckon themselves very meritorious and magnanimous
for it. Quite recently in the presence of a vast English audience,
and by a countryman of mine whose genial spirit, unsurpassed
genius and wondrous eloquence on an unlimited variety of topics
are admitted and admired wherever he is known, no little credit
was claimed for our Northern acquiescence in this Pro-Slavery
interpretation. Alas, for the morals and religion, which adjust
themselves to such an interpretation, and are made to harmonize
with the diabolical wickedness it calls for! I add in this connec-

tion, that so far from there being a law for Slavery in the Constitution, there can be no law for it either in or out of the Constitution. Law is for the protection of rights. But Slavery strikes down every right. All would be quick to scout the idea of a law for murder. But Slavery being worse than murder, they should be quicker to scout the possibility of a law for Slavery. I say *worse* than murder. For what enlightened parent would not rather see his child in the grave of the murdered than in bondage to the slaveholder? It is too late for a civilized nation to admit the possibility of the legalization of Slavery. It should be held that the nation, which any longer admits it, does thereby put itself outside the pale of civilization. But surely I did not need to speak to a British audience of the impossibility of legalizing Slavery. How truthfully, eloquently, and grandly your own Brougham said: "Tell me not of rights. Talk not of the property of the planter in his slaves. I deny the rights. I acknowledge not the property. The principles, the feelings of our common nature rise in rebellion against it. Be the appeal made to the understanding or to the heart, the sentence is the same that rejects it. In vain you tell me of laws that sanction such a claim. There is a law above all the enactments of human codes. It is the law written by the finger of God upon the heart of man: and by that law unchangeable and eternal while men despise fraud and loathe rapine and abhor blood they shall reject with indignation THE WILD AND GUILTY FANTASY THAT MAN CAN HOLD PROPERTY IN MAN."

I have now asked on what grounds it is that Britons sympathize with the greatest and guiltiest Rebellion the world ever knew:—a Rebellion the sole grievance for which was that there was not scope enough for Slavery. And I have now disclaimed two grounds for your sympathy with my country in her resistance to this Rebellion. The way then is open for me to state the only ground on which I claim the world's sympathy with my country in this resistance. This only ground is THE SACREDNESS OF NATIONALITY. An eminent British statesman has, within the last year, declared that "the South is fighting for independence and the North for empire." The North was offended at the declaration. But it should not have been. Your statesman is right. For one I readily accepted his statement. The South *is* fighting for independence—an independence, however, which she has no right to. The North *is* fighting for empire: and it is not only a lawful empire but one which she is under the highest obligations to fight for. In a twofold sense is it *empire* for which she fights— since she is intent both on the restoration of all the national boundaries and on the restoration of the government commensurate with all those boundaries. I repeat it, the only ground on which I claim the world's sympathy with my suffering country is the sacredness of nationality. The family relation is sacred, and must not be violated. A family may of its own accord break up and scatter. But this must not be forced upon it. Nationality is also

inviolable.   Nations may agree with each other to change their
boundaries.   But the change must not be forced upon them.   All
families must leave each family to live : and all nations must leave
each nation to live.   The family and the nation—or, as I might
say, the literal and the national family—are the two institutions of
earth whose permanence all families in the one case and all nations
in the other should foster and rejoice in.   These institutions are
too precious to be violated or neglected.   Far too large a share of
human happiness and human hopes is indissolubly connected with
them to allow such violation or neglect.   For ninety years the
Poles have been without a nation.   What arithmetic can compute
their sufferings during these ninety years !   As I was gazing, the
other day, upon the picture of the beautiful and sublime face of
an eminent Polish exile, I fancied that the sorrows of a whole
nation were expressed in that one face of utter sadness.   How
murderous was the cruelty, which robbed the Poles of nationality!
How far worse than every other form of orphanage was that to
which it reduced them !   And they still suffer as in the freshness
of their suffering.   Italy too still bleeds under her dismember-
ment.   And would you, or any of you, in order to gratify a handful of slaveholders, who are compelling their poor, ignorant, and
know-not-what-they-do neighbors to fight for Slavery—and would
you, I say, for this miserable and guilty purpose, have the hearts
of my countrymen also wrung with the agonies of a broken-up
nation—of a nation, whose physical features show that her North
and her South, whatever you may say of her East and West, can
never be parted from each other but by a war upon nature as well
as upon nationality ?   Oh! when will nations cease from the meanness
and wickedness of wronging each other ?   How mean and wicked
to fall upon the peace and rights of a family !   Immeasurably
more so to fall upon the peace and rights of a nation.   Nations
must cease to be jealous of each other.   They must stand by
each other, and never sympathize with an assault upon nationality, ·
unless it be in that rare case where the assault is for the redress of
wrongs so flagrant and unendurable, that nothing can be sacred
enough to stand in the way of their redress.   And then every
nation should remember, that it behooves her, for her own safety,
to be true to other nations.   If England shall, in this hour of my
country's calamity, go to the side of my country's enemies, is
there not great danger that she will thereby provoke my country
to go to the side of England's enemies when England shall in her
turn be overtaken by the like calamity ?

If I know myself, I would deeply sympathize with England,
should a part of her Counties take up arms to dismember her.
I would call it right in that case to fight for " empire": and indeed I know no nation that would in such case fight more earnestly for it.   Wouldn't you call it right ?   Nay, wouldn't even
the eminent statesman, who *reproached* my country with fighting
for " empire," call it right for England, if in the circumstances of
my country, to fight for " empire" ?   But if England would be en-

titled to sympathy in her endeavors to reduce to loyalty her revolting Counties, why is not my country entitled to it in her struggle
with revolting States ? It is true that the States, which make up
my nation, are more important political divisions than the Counties
of England—for they are larger, have more administrative power,
and have legislative power also. Nevertheless an American
State no more than an English County is a nation ; and has no
more right than an English County to set up for itself.

Britain, France, America, and all the nations of the earth should
be faithful to each other, and should spare their sympathies for objects worthier than piracies and slaveholding ambition and slaveholding greed. The Rebellion in my country is nothing more nor
less than Slavery in arms. The monster had for many years
tried to accomplish his infernal objects through the ballot-box and
through all sorts of intrigue and corruption. Failing of entire
success by these means, he took up arms. But, thank God, the
Rebellion is fast going down. Slavery, being identical with it, of
course goes down with it. The ending of the Rebellion will necessarily be the ending of Slavery. Not one shred of Slavery
will survive the utter extinction of the Rebellion. And let none
fear that it will be anywhere reëstablished. The people, who
have once thrown off Slavery, will never recall it. They will
have no desire to exchange the blessings of Liberty for the curse
of Slavery. Your West-India planters continued, after the Decree
of Emancipation, to ask for more money and more favors: but
none of them wanted the restoration of Slavery. They had all
had enough of that.

Yes, its self-inflicted wound is mortal, and American Slavery must
soon die. When it is dead, then, as I trust, will my countrymen,
North and South, East and West, having through this war worked
out in tears and blood the heavy and Heaven-appointed penalty of
their crimes against the black man, penitently and unitedly engage
in redressing his matchless wrongs, healing the deep gashes in his
spirit, and opening the way wide and generous for his bodily,
mental and moral improvement. If this shall come to pass, then
will a nation grow up in my land grander and more beautiful than
any other nation. This will not be because we are better than
other people—for we are not. It will be because nature has dealt
more bountifully with us than with any other land. And then
will my nation, because it shall have become just to its own people of all classes, conditions, and complexions, be relied on, the
earth over, to be just to all nations. For, with the change of
but one word, we can say to a nation with all the confidence and
emphasis with which your greatest of all poets said to an individual :

"To thine own self be true :
And it must follow, as the day the night,
Thou canst not then be false to any *nation*."

ON THE COUNTRY.

LETTER TO HON. D. C. LITTLEJOHN.

PETERBORO, January 14th, 1864.

HON. MR. LITTLEJOHN, M. C.:

DEAR SIR: In common with your other constituents, I lament your sickness. May you soon regain your health, and the country soon regain your services! This is emphatically a time when the country needs to have every one of her true and intelligent friends at his post.

July 22d, 1861, the House of Representatives adopted with but two dissenting voices, Mr. Crittenden's Resolution, a part of which is that: "This war is waged but to defend and maintain the supremacy of the Constitution, and to preserve the Union with all the dignity, equality, and rights of the several States unimpaired; and that as soon as those objects are accomplished the war ought to cease."

This resolution is in my judgment the greatest and most pernicious of all our mistakes in carrying on the war. From the day of its passage it has never ceased to furnish the Seymours and other enemies of the Administration with their most plausible and effective arguments against the Administration, and with their mightiest influences to obstruct and pervert the war. The resolution declares war for the Constitution and Union—which it should not have done; and it fails to declare war against the rebels—which alone it should have done. No wonder that with so bad a beginning the nation has not even yet carried on an unconditional war against them! — and no wonder therefore that the war has been so protracted! Should a portion of her people revolt, England would feel that here was something to declare war *against*. She would find no time and feel no disposition to declare war *for* any thing—not even for her chosen form of government—no, nor even for her existence. She would address herself to the one work of subduing the revolt, cost however much it might to what she most cherished. She would go forward to conquer or perish. Very precious, indeed, the interests she would leave behind her. But she would no more suffer them to interfere with the absorbing object before her than would Cortes have suffered his ships to tempt his little army with the possibilities of a safe retreat. He burnt his ships; and she would call for no stipulations in behalf of those interests. To save our Constitution and Union has been our chief object (real and pretended) in this war. Whereas our sole object in it should have been to crush the Rebellion—and this too at whatever needful expense even to the Constitution or the Union. In saying this, I surely do not expose myself to the charge of undervaluing either Constitution or Union. For who has written and spoken more than I have for the Constitution, just as it is?—and who has accepted more constantly and cordially all the terms of the Union?

A wise and firm father resolves, uncalculatingly and unconditionally, to put down his rebellious child. If reminded that his family may thereby be broken up, his reply is, that, family or no family, the young rebel shall go down. So too the brave household whom the burglar awakes, will, if told by him to see to their safety, prefer, at whatever hazard to their safety, to see to his capture. And why a nation act upon a different principle? No other nation, in the circumstances of ours, ever did. No other nation, ancient or modern, ever furnished a parallel at this point to the conduct of our own. A Rebellion, the most gigantic the world ever saw—the most guilty too, since its only real plea was that under the Constitution there were not sufficient scope and provision for the safety, extension, and perpetuity of Slavery—broke out against us. Our one and unconditional work was to put it down. No part of this work was it to save Constitution, Union, or Nation. Nay, if, in our struggle to put it down, all these shall perish, their never-to-perish monument would be worth infinitely more to the glory of God and the good of man, than could their salvation if achieved by compromise or indirection. Very sacred is nationality. But our sense of its sacredness is shown far less in trying to save a nation than in trying to punish, though at whatever hazard to the nation, the miscreants, who are at work to destroy it.

And now whence comes it that our nation has, at this point, behaved so unlike every other nation? Whence comes it that when heaven and earth bade it crush the Rebellion, and at whatever cost and without any condition or calculation—whence comes it, I ask, that it turned away from the one and only work it had to do to listen to the traitorous cry: "Save the Constitution: Save the Union!" It comes, I reply, from the simple fact that, from the first, the American people have been artfully, industriously, constantly trained to worship the Constitution and the Union. And what is it that has so successfully called for this training? It is Slavery. By day and by night Slavery has worked to make the American people worshipers of the Constitution and the Union—urging, all the time, its lying claim that the Constitution and the Union were made to uphold, extend, and perpetuate Slavery. Only a short and entirely natural step was it to their becoming worshipers of Slavery itself. And, because they took that step, the

American people have not yet been able to stand up to a square
fight against the Rebellion. For the Rebellion is simply Slavery
in arms ; and to their deluded minds Slavery, whether armed or unarmed, being the very pet and cosset of the Constitution and
Union, is as much to be cherished and protected as the Constitution and Union. The enemy paralyzed the Egyptians when
he succeeded in placing between them and himself on the battle-
field their sacred animals. And why our people could not strike
promptly and unreservedly at the Rebellion, was simply because
sacred Slavery stood between it and them. You well remember that
the first concern of our early Commanders in this war was to provide for the safety of Slavery. Nothing had been seen more insane
or ridiculous since the days when an Egyptian army made more
account of saving the worshiped cat or crocodile than of conquering the enemy.

Let me refer to some of the evil results of this Congressional Resolution of July 22d, 1861, which, as its first and unquoted part
shows, was intended to be a resolution of safety to Slavery instead
of destruction to the Rebellion. It estops Congress from complaining of the over-zealous and one-idea Abolitionist, who withholds his hand from the work of putting down the Rebellion unconditionally. It licenses him to substitute for that work the upholding of the Constitution and Union. Moreover, as it virtually
licenses him to take his own Abolition way for upholding them, it
must not complain if that shall prove an unwise and even wild way.
It also estops Congress from complaining of the Pro-Slavery Democrats for their incessant clogging of the wheels of war with
their affected cautions for the safety of the Constitution and the
Union. For it has itself supplanted the only true issue—the sole
and stern issue of the nation with the Rebellion—by a paramount
concern for the Constitution and the Union. It is in the name of
this very concern that the Seymours and Woods are at work to
consummate the ruin of our Republic, and to build up a slaveholding oligarchy which will be grateful to all, North as well as
South, who, like themselves, love the distinctions of Aristocracy and
hate the level of Democracy.

Would that Congress had not taken a ground, which allows certain men to pretend to be against the rebels, when they are not!
Would that Congress had declared war against the rebels, and so
compelled these certain men to stand forth openly for or against
the war! Nay, would that Congress might now, even at this late
day, summon the courage to make a clean, unconditional, uncompromising declaration of war—a declaration which shall be *for*
nothing ; and which shall be *against* the rebels, and against nothing else.

"The Reconstruction of the Government!" For one I am sorry
that the public mind should be prematurely occupied with the subject. From the day when the Rebellion began, the nation should
have been concerned about nothing else than to put it down ; and
I add, that until it is put down the nation should be concerned

about nothing else than to put it down. We are not so strong and so entirely certain of success that we can afford to be divided amongst ourselves by premature issues. Moreover, we shall not know what will be our duty to the conquered South until we shall have conquered her, and seen in what temper the conquest leaves her. As we advance into the enemy's territory, let it be subjected to a military or other temporary government; and when, if ever, the whole territory shall be ours, then let the terms of a Treaty of Peace, and not a mere Proclamation, say whether the governments and constitutions of that territory shall be as they were before, or shall be so modified as to meet any reasonable demands for their modification. That the Treaty of Peace will have no right to modify them is absurd. That the Constitution will stand in the way of it is ridiculous. When half a nation arms itself against the other half, and throws off the common Constitution, it is for that other half, if victorious, to choose whether it will or will not treat the conquered rebels according to the Constitution. It may, at its own option, treat them as rebels, or as it would foreign enemies. In such circumstances it is bound by no code nor Constitution. It is a law unto itself; and in the light of that law it is to decide what the national welfare calls for. I am free to say that I would have the Treaty revive all the conquered States, and all those rights to which they were formerly entitled under the Constitution. I say it, because I would that they might be found worthy of it. But to repose such confidence in those States, were they still impenitent and revengeful, and waiting and longing for another opportunity to strike at the heart of the nation, would be madness; and would be an immeasurable wrong as well toward the conquered as toward the conquerors. The conquered States will be entitled to nothing in virtue of their rights under their former relations. What they have done to break up these relations, (the North is entirely innocent of any thing to this end,) has worked the forfeiture of all those rights. In the name, however, of wisdom as well as humanity, let the Treaty accord to them all that it would be safe for them and for us to have accorded. Let it restore to them gladly and lovingly, all the rights of sister States, provided only that, in a sound view of the circumstances, prudence shall not forbid so entire a restoration.

I expressed my preference for a Treaty of Peace. It was proper that Washington should proclaim on what terms a local insurrection in Pennsylvania might be pacified and ended. But I would not leave it even to a Washington to decide on what terms the two halves of a mighty nation should make peace with each other.

The Proclamations! Our President is both a strong and an honest man. Moreover, his patriotic heart is firmly set on subduing the Rebellion. Nevertheless, even he, as well as other men, may fall into errors. I do not complain that his Proclamation of Freedom did not cover all the slaves. It covered as many as in his convictions the exigencies of war allowed him to declare free; and he

5

certainly had no moral right to extend his Proclamation beyond
these convictions. In his civil capacity he could not liberate a
single slave ; and in his military capacity he could liberate only so
many as there was a military necessity for liberating. What I do
complain of is his recognition of the right of the Supreme Court to
pass upon that Proclamation. This Court has not the right to say
whether it is or is not valid and operative ; and I would that Congress might protest unanimously and most solemnly against the
President's recognition of it. Let this Court, if it please, take into
its hands whatever Proclamations the President may make in his
civil capacity. But in regard to all those which he puts forth as
Head of the Army, I would say to it : "Hands off!" It is true
that it is the Constitution, of which this Court is the acknowledged
interpreter, which makes the President the Head of the Army.
But it is also true that it is the LAW OF WAR and not the Constitution, which tells him what he may do in that capacity. What
if among his military orders should be one to poison the springs
and wells and food in the enemy's territory !— would our country
submit to it, in case the Supreme Court should sanction it ? None
the less because of that sanction would our whole country along with
the whole civilized world rise up against the barbarous order.
Surely, surely this Court needs no encouragement to enlarge its
powers. The Dred Scott case is of itself sufficient to prove that
its tendency is to set no limits to those powers.

Hundreds of thousands are petitioning Congress to abolish what
remains of American Slavery. The "Confiscation and Emancipation Bill" left comparatively little of it ; and then came the President's Proclamation to make even that little less. I hope Congress
will grant the petition. There are some persons who hold that
Congress can, as a civil measure, enact the abolition of Slavery—
and this, too, without providing any indemnity. There are also
some who hold that there can be no legal Slavery under a Constitution which requires "a republican form of government" in all the
States, and also requires that "no person shall be deprived of
life, liberty, or property, without due process of law." And there
are some persons of such extreme views as to hold that Slavery,
being the matchless crime against God and man, can no more than
murder itself, be legalized by any Constitution, or embodied in any
real law. But I could wish that Congress might avoid all these
questions and abolish Slavery as a war measure, and accompany
the abolition with a suitable indemnity to loyal slaveholders.

I notice that the plans for military canals are already coming
before Congress, and that an objection to building the canal around
Niagara Falls is much urged. It is a taking one, inasmuch as it
appeals to local interests and individual selfishness. This objection
is, that Western produce, when once afloat on Lake Ontario, will
descend the St. Lawrence, and thus be lost to our cities. And is
this an objection? Most certainly, the race of bad logicians is not
yet extinct. In the first place, the Government does not propose
to build these canals for commerce, but for military protection and

advantage. And in the next place, if the Niagara Canal shall give to the immense agricultural West a better market on the St. Lawrence than it can have in Boston, New-York, or Philadelphia, then ought the whole nation to rejoice in the prospect of the building of that Canal. To get better prices for its produce is of infinitely greater importance to our country than to keep undiminished a few branches of trade in a few of its cities. Because I have some land in your Oswego, I naturally desire to have a share of the vessels laden with Western produce turn into that city, and so benefit her as well as Boston and New-York. But it would be very selfish and mean in me to desire this if the produce can find a better market on the St. Lawrence. Rather should I say, let Oswego be deserted; and let Montreal outgrow New-York, if she can do so by attracting the produce and increasing the wealth of our farmers. But I apprehend that the great West will be sadly disappointed, if she expects by means of the Niagara Canal to have a better market on the St. Lawrence, which for half the year is closed with ice, than she can have elsewhere. If this is her expectation from that Canal, then so far she is unwise in calling for the building of it. The Canal will be an important military work; but it will bring comparatively little to the markets of Canada.

And I also notice, that there is a movement in Congress to terminate the Reciprocity Treaty—that Treaty which, you remember, I worked so hard for when I was a Member of Congress. I hope that my country will not be guilty of the illiberality and unsound political economy of refusing to exchange natural productions with any country. The complaint is, that Canada sells too much to us. But if she is profited by selling to us, so are we by buying of her. If the lumberman in Maine can not get as much for his lumber under the "Reciprocity Treaty," there is nevertheless a full equivalent in the fact that the builder in Ohio buys his Canada lumber far cheaper because of that Treaty. If it is a gain to sell dear, so it is also a gain to buy cheap. We have now free access to the vast and rich forests of Canada. What a folly to cut ourselves off from this advantage for the miserable reason that Canada enjoys a corresponding advantage! — that whilst we reap the profit of buying her lumber, she reaps the profit of selling it to us! But it is held that the price of our wheat, as well as of our lumber, is reduced by this Canada competition. Can it, however, make any material difference to our farmers, whether the Canada wheat goes to Liverpool by the St. Lawrence or by New-York and Boston? Both our country and Canada grow a surplus of wheat; and hence, in the case of both, the price is regulated by the foreign market. Canada wheat will come into competition with ours, whether we do or do not continue to enjoy the advantage of transporting it across our country. Why then should we surrender this advantage? And it is also held that free Canada coal cheapens the price of ours. The more the better, declare reason and humanity! And in response to this declaration, all the people, including especially the shivering poor, cry: "Amen!"

I close with inquiring who they are that clamor for Tariffs and the termination of the "Reciprocity Treaty"? They are few else than the comparative handful, who desire higher prices for what they have to sell. The masses, and especially the poor who make up so large a share of the masses, desire low prices. In, then, their name and behalf let us favor, not the policy which makes dear, but that which makes cheap, the necessaries of life!

Your friend,   GERRIT SMITH.

LETTER TO HON. PRESTON KING.

• ◆ • —

PETERBORO, January 29th, 1864.

HON. PRESTON KING:

DEAR SIR: It was your and my privilege to meet, a day or two since, with a number of intelligent gentlemen, and to exchange views with them. It was gratifying to find them all so faithful to the Constitution, the Union, and the country, and therefore so intent on crushing the Rebellion.

I was, however, not a little surprised and sorry to find that they were, generally, very sensitive in regard to criticisms on the Government. For instance, although they were ready to say that it is our right to prosecute the war as well under the Law of War as under the Constitution, they, nevertheless, shrunk from saying that nothing in the Constitution on attainder, or on any thing else, should be plead in mitigation of the penalties incurred by the rebels. Why did they shrink from it? Simply because the President, whose few mistakes are as nothing compared with his good and grand deeds, had put in such a plea, and Congress had accepted it. But it never should have been put in nor accepted. How false, even ludicrously false, our position in consequence of this misstep of the Government! We take away his property from the armed rebel. We want to shoot him. But if we do shoot him, the property passes away from us! And thus have we tempted ourselves to spare him! The simple truth is, that we have not only all, but more than all, the rights of war against the rebels that we have against a foreign enemy. For the Constitution, which the rebels have flung away, but which we still hold over them, arms us with punishments beyond those provided for by the International Code of War.

Still more did these gentlemen shrink from saying that it is hazardous to the welfare of the masses, and fearfully violative of the great and sacred majority principle, on which rests Republican Government, to authorize a comparative handful to mould, and impose upon a State, a *permanent* form of government. The President, however, had authorized it, and hence, in the esteem of those gentlemen, the measure was put beyond criticism. I say nothing against providing, in whatever way, a *temporary* government, to meet the exigencies of war. But peace alone can afford the composure and advantages which are necessary to devise and mature a *permanent* form of government. Let me here add, that the Constitution, with its every line and letter, should be dear to us all. But the majority principle is its very soul; and hence, to violate it is to strike at the existence of the Constitution. One effect of authorizing this little minority to construct a *permanent* form of government will be to shut out the black man from the ballot-box. But as freedom and arms are to be granted to him, there will be neither peace nor safety in the land until the right of suffrage is also granted to him.

I could not fail to see that, on the occasion referred to, I made myself quite offensive by calling in question the infallibility of the Government. My faithfulness to it was construed into unfaithfulness to it. My exception to a couple of its measures was scarcely distinguishable from the vulgar attacks upon it. But there should be great patience with the proved friend of his Government when he finds fault with it. For, at the most, it is but misjudgments of which he is guilty. Moreover, his misjudgments may, after all, turn out to be sound judgments. Multitudes, once hostile to my life-long principles, I have lived to see become identified with them. And ere they are aware, those who dissent from my present positions, may have come round to them. By the way, the popular notion that our able and upright Administration is weakened by whatever criticisms upon its measures, is far from true. To such of these criticisms as are made in the spirit of candor and patriotism it is ever ready to listen, and, therefore, is it enlightened and strengthened by whatever of wisdom there may be in them.

The President, when admitting, in regard to some of his measures, that they are not final and unalterable, virtually invites his fellow-citizens to suggest changes in them. He was wrong in referring it to the Supreme Court instead of the Law of War to decide whether Proclamations, which he had issued as Head of the Army, and therefore under the Law of War, are valid or invalid :— and let us be honest and courageous enough to say so. Again, he was wrong in holding that certain penalties, which we can inflict under the Law of War, must, of necessity, be reduced by the Constitution :—and at this point also let us deal faithfully with him.

Our Administration is indeed badly off, if, whilst on the one hand its enemies are assailing it for the purpose of destroying it, its friends, on the other, may not criticise it for the sake of helping it.

One thing more. We should adjourn to the latest possible day all causes and occasions of division amongst ourselves. Divisions in the presence of our enemy, who is mighty because he is desperate, are dangerous to the last degree. Now, the tendency of naming persons for the Presidency is to produce these divisions. Hence, there should be no nominations of President before midsummer, by which time, the Rebellion being ended, such divisions would be harmless.

Party in time of Peace is right. But in time of War it is wrong—in effect, treasonably wrong. I hoped that the Republicans had given up Party. But in the interview to which I referred at the beginning of this letter, I felt that perhaps they had not.

With great regard, your friend,

GERRIT SMITH.

GERRIT SMITH

ON THE

REBELLION.

— ••• -

VOLUME II.

SPEECHES AND LETTERS

OF

GERRIT SMITH

(FROM JANUARY, 1864, TO JANUARY, 1865)

ON THE

REBELLION.

VOLUME II.

New-York:
AMERICAN NEWS COMPANY,
121 NASSAU STREET.

1865.

ON THE CONSTITUTION.

—— • • ——

War goes beyond Constitutional Restrictions.
Down with the Rebellion at Whatever Cost to the Constitution.
"The Body is more than Raiment!" The Country is more than the Constitution.
Time now for nothing but to Crush the Rebellion.

—— • • ——

To My Neighbors :

"DAMN the Constitution!" said one in the hearing of myself and several others. I had always disliked profanity: and I had always honored the Constitution—welcoming every part of it. Nevertheless this exclamation was music in my ears. Why was it? It was because of the connection and spirit in which it burst from the speaker. He was arguing with rapid and fervid eloquence that the Government should ply every possible means for the speediest crushing of the rebellion—when a listening Conservative threw in the qualification : "But all according to the Constitution!" No wonder that the speaker could not brook this interruption. No wonder that an oath should leap forth to attest the indignation of his patriotic soul. It was not contempt for the Constitution, but displeasure at the thrusting of it in his way, which prompted the profanity. Had it been the Bible itself, that was thus impertinently cited, an oath might still have been the consequence.

In a past century a New-England Puritan, in order to reconcile his black boy to the periodical whippings he gave him, said : "I whip you for the good of your soul." To which the sufferer very naturally replied : "I wish I had n't a soul!" Often during this War has the excessively tender and untimely care for the Constitution tempted me to wish that we had n't a Constitution. Thus was I tempted when, July 22, 1861, the House of Representatives, instead of manfully resolving that the War was for putting down the Rebellion and for nothing else, meanly resolved that it was for maintaining the supremacy of the Constitution. Thus was I tempted when Congress, a year or two ago, was ridiculously employed in looking into the Constitution to learn how far it might confiscate the possessions of the millions who were striking at the life of the nation. I notice that, now again, Congress is, in this same connection, twattling about the Constitution. Thus was

I tempted when the President left it to the Judges, or, in other
words, to the Constitution, to say whether Proclamations, which
he had issued as Head of the Army, should be allowed to stand.
Unhappiest and most contemptible of all nations are we, if whilst
every other nation can carry on war with all the latitude of the
law of war—of the law of necessity and of self-preservation, we
are to be "cabined, cribbed, confined" by a mere paper. Infinitely
better that we had no Constitution than that we should have one,
which is allowed to fetter our freedom and restrict our choice of
means in time of war.

By the way, the most cheering instance of resistance to this
practice of supplanting the law of war with the Constitution is
the recent disclaimer of the Supreme Court, in Vallandigham's
case, of authority to review the proceedings of a military commission.

Never yet have we carried on an unconditional and square fight
with the rebels: and never can we until we shall have the political and moral courage to resent and rise above the endeavors of
demagogues and sympathizers with the rebels to embarrass our
conduct of the war by these impertinent constitutional questions.
But these questions are not the only hinderance in the way of the
only proper mode of warfare. Another and not less serious hinderance has sprung up in the untimely agitation of the question:
"Who shall be the next President?" It is fearful to think how
mighty are the electioneering influences, which will now be set at
work by office-holders, office-seekers, army contractors, and many
other classes. It is fearful to think how wide-spread and deep a concern there will be to conduct the War, not so as to end the rebellion and save the country, but so as to promote party and individual interests. It is fearful to think of the possible extent and character of the divisions that may now be wrought amongst ourselves
—divisions that may do more than the enemy can do to destroy our
beloved country. Who shall be the next President, should not have
been spoken of before midsummer. The New-York *Independent*
says it should only have been thought of. But it should not even
have been thought of before that time. In the judgment of this
journal, to be thinking from this early day of the Presidential
Election—"to be prudently considering it"—to "ponder" it—
would be the people's best preparation for acting wisely in it.
But their unspeakably better preparation would be to forget the
whole subject for the coming four or five months, and to be during
all that time united as one man in wiping out the last remains of
the accursed Rebellion. Such a perfect union for such a righteous end would be their best possible education for selecting none
but a fit man for the Presidency.

Quite a natural fruit of this premature agitation of the Presidential question is it, that there are already on the one hand Union
men who are slandering and vilifying Abraham Lincoln, and on
the other hand Union men who will not tolerate even the most
generous and friendly criticism on any of his views and measures.

And still another hinderance has been thrown in our way. The proposition to amend the Constitution tends to produce divisions amongst ourselves, and to divert us from that one work which should absorb us—the work of crushing the Rebellion. It is said that for the safety of posterity and to prevent the recurrence of the Rebellion we must have a constitutional prohibition of Slavery. I reply that we can not afford to attend to posterity now—that our own case needs all our present attention. It will be time enough to amend the Constitution after we shall have ended the Rebellion. The leisure which peace affords, is necessary to devise and adopt amendments of that precious paper. I do not object to the abolishing of Slavery. No sooner had slavery fired at Sumter, than emancipation should have fired at slavery. And this, too, Constitution or no Constitution for it. It was our right, because our necessity, to kill that which aimed to kill the nation. At no time since the War began should Congress have delayed to abolish by force of its war power every remnant of slavery:— dealing generously at the same time with loyal slaveholders.

Moreover, as to guarding posterity from slavery, and therefore from a war for slavery, I would say, that the land once cleared of it, slavery will never again be set up in it. Slavery is an abomination which the people, who have once got rid of it, are never disposed to recall. It is a disease, which no people take a second time. The French learned this lesson in their mad attempt to reenslave the Haytiens. When, a few years ago, Spain grasped San Domingo, she promised the Dominicans not to introduce slavery. The promise was superfluous. The Dominicans will take care to protect themselves from slavery and from Spain also. Constitutional provisions against slavery will not avail to keep out slavery from the Southern States: but the freedom and the arms we are giving to their slaves will. Where a people want slavery, they will have it, whatever the Constitution. Our Constitution is against slavery. But the people wanted slavery. To say the least, they felt interested in consenting to it. Hence they fell in with the pro-slavery interpretation of the Constitution. Good men fell in with it because it was the prevailing interpretation. I said that our Constitution is against slavery. Certainly it is:— for it says, "No person shall be deprived of life, liberty, or property without due process of law:" and "No State shall pass any bill of attainder." But slavery is the most emphatic and abominable attainder. And it says too: "The United States *shall* guarantee to every State in the Union a Republican form of government." Has South-Carolina, where a handful of tyrants own three fifths of all the people, a *Republican* form of government? Surely we can not admit it without being ashamed that our nation has a Republican name.

I close with the remark, that now is not the time either to improve the Constitution or to be solicitous to save it; that now is not the time, much as they are needed, to be building roads to the Pacific, or indeed to be making any expenditures or embarking in

any projects, whose results will not be early enough to help us
in this War ; and that not only now is not the time for President-
making but not the time to maintain the Democratic party, nor
to revive the Republican party and seek thereby to harness to a
platform built four years ago and in far other circumstances a
nation which is solving, through seas of tears and blood, the question of her life or death.   I thought that the Republican party
was disbanded.   The assurances that it was—were they mistaken
or deceitful ?   Tens of thousands of men, not Republicans, have
worked with Republicans to put down the Rebellion.   But they
can not turn away from that work to any other :—nor can they
consent to couple with it the building up of the Republican or
any other party.

PETERBORO, February 24, 1864.

ON THE FORT PILLOW AND PLYMOUTH MASSACRES.

——• • •——

The Immediate Criminals not always the only Criminals.
The Creators of a Wicked Public Sentiment responsible for its Fruits.
Patriotism, and not Party Politics, our Present Need.
No Taxes too heavy, if needed to Put Down the Rebellion.

——• • •——

THE whole civilized world will be startled and horrified by this slaughter of probably not less than five or six hundred persons. The excuse in the case of a part of the slaughtered is, that they were traitorous citizens of the Confederacy: in the case of another part, that they were whites fighting by the side of blacks: in the case of the remainder, including women and even children, that they were blacks. That these were blacks, was cause enough why, though numbering three or four hundred, they should be murdered—murdered in utter contempt of all the sacred rights of prisoners of war. It is of the crime against these, I would now speak.

Who are to be held amenable for this crime? The rebels. Yes, but not the rebels only. The authorship of this crime, so matchless in its worst features, is very comprehensive. The responsibility for it is wider than our nation. England shares in the authorship and responsibility, because it was she who planted slavery in America, and because it is slavery out of which this crime has come. Our own nation, however, is the far guiltier one. The guilt of this crime is upon all her people who have contributed to that public sentiment, which releases white men from respecting the rights of black men. Our highest Court says that this satanic sentiment prevailed in the early existence of our nation. Certain it is, that it has prevailed in all the later periods of that existence. Who are they who have contributed to generate it? All who have held that blacks are unfit to sit by the side of whites in the church, the school, the car and at the table. All who have been in favor of making his complexion shut out a black man from the ballot-box. All who have been for making a man's title to any of the rights of manhood turn on the color of the skin in which his Maker has chosen to wrap him. All, in short, who have hated or despised the black man.

Even President Lincoln, whom God now blesses and will yet more bless for the much he has done for his black brethren, is not entire-

ly innnocent of the Fort Pillow and Plymouth massacres. Had
his plan of "Reconstruction" recognized the right of the black
men to vote, it would thereby have contributed to lift them up
above outrage, instead of contributing, as it now does, to invite
outrage upon them. By the way, it is a pity that he undertook
"Reconstruction." It was entirely beyond his civil capacity to do
so: and it was entirely beyond his military capacity to have a part
in setting up any other than a military or provisional government.
Moreover, this is the only kind of government which it is proper
to set up in the midst of war. The leisure and advantages of
peace are necessary in the great and difficult work of establishing
a permanent government. In this connection let me advert for a
moment to the doctrine, "Once a State always a State"—a doctrine so frequently wielded against "Reconstruction" on any
terms. Where is the authority for this doctrine? In the Constitution, it is said. But nowhere does the Constitution say that a
State may plunge into war, secure at all hazards from some of the
penalties of war. But amongst the penalties of war is whatever
change the conqueror may choose to impose upon the conquered
territory. I admit that it is very desirable to have all the revolting States reëstablished—reïnstated. But that there is any law by
which this becomes inevitable is absurd. Nowhere does the Constitution say that a State is to be exempt from the operation of
the law of war. Nowhere does it undertake to override the law
of war. How clear is it, then, that by this paramount law these
revolted States will, when conquered, lie at the will of the conqueror! And how clear is it, that it will then turn not at all
upon the Constitution, but upon this will of the conqueror,
backed by this paramount law of war, whether the old statehood
of these States shall be revived, or whether they shall be remanded to a territorial condition, and put upon their good be-
havior!

There is another instance in which the President has contributed to that cruel public sentiment, which leaves the black race un-
protected. I refer to his so strangely long delay in promising protection to the black soldier, and to the even longer and not yet
ended delay in affording it. The President is a humane as well
as an honest man; and the only explanation I can find for his delay to protect the black soldier and to put an end, so far as in him
lies, to the various, innumerable, incessant outrages upon the freed-
men is in the continuance of his childish and cowardly desire to
conciliate his native Kentucky and the Democratic party.

I argued that even President Lincoln is responsible in some degree for that public sentiment, which invites outrage upon the black
man and leaves him a prey to the wicked. Those Members of Congress, who are opposing the reasonable measure of letting the black
man vote in the Territories, are also guilty of favoring that public
sentiment which broke out in the crime at Fort Pillow and Plymouth. Similarly guilty are those members who would make the
pay of a black soldier less than that of a white one. And so are

those members who consent to leave a fugitive slave statute in existence. In a word, all should tax their consciences with the sin of this public sentiment and with the resulting crime at Fort Pillow and Plymouth, whose influence, by either word or deed, has been to keep up in this heathen land the caste-spirit—that preeminent characteristic of heathenism. I call this a heathen land. To the Christ-Religion—that simple religion of equal rights and of doing as you would be done by—there can be no greater insult than to call a nation in which, as in this, the most cruel and murderous caste-spirit prevails, a Christian nation.

Both on the right hand and on the left, I hear that our nation is to be saved. But my fears that it will not, often become very strong. That the Rebellion is to be crushed, I deeply believe. Often in the course of Providence a wicked people, which is itself to be afterward destroyed, is previously to be used in destroying another and generally more wicked people. There are striking illustrations of this in the Bible. The duty of abolitionists and anti-abolitionists, Democrats and Republicans, to work unitedly, incessantly, and unconditionally for the overthrow of the Rebellion I have not only never doubted, but ever urged. I hold it to be unpatriotic and even traitorous for the Abolitionists to make any conditions in behalf of their specialty, and to propose, as some of them do, to go against the Rebellion only so far as going against it will be going against slavery. So too are those Democrats unpatriotic and even traitorous who can favor the War, only under the stipulation that it be so conducted as to harm neither the Democratic party nor the Constitution. To put down the Rebellion is an object immeasurably higher than to save a party or to save the Constitution, or even to save the country. No man is right-minded, who would not have it put down, even though it be at the expense of the last man and the last dollar.

If any thing makes me doubt that the Rebellion will be crushed it is the omission of Congress to abolish slavery, now when it is so clearly seen that the abolition of slavery is an indispensable means to the abolition of the Rebellion. The proposed Amendment to the Constitution I take no interest in. One reason why I do not, is, that it is not a proposition to abolish slavery *now*. Another is, that war is not the time to be tinkering at constitutions. I see it denied that Congress has the power, even as a war measure, to abolish slavery. Amazing delusion! There is in every nation an absolute power for carrying on war. The nation that disclaims it may as well give up being a nation. In our own, this power is vested in Congress. Congress is to declare war: and Congress is " to make all laws necessary and proper (itself of course the sole judge of the necessity and propriety) for carrying into execution" the declaration. Is it the institution of apprenticeship, which it finds to be in the way of the successful prosecution of the war?—then is it to sweep it out of the way. Is it the abomination of slavery?—then is it to strike at that.

There is, however, one thing more which sometimes, though not

often, raises a doubt in me whether the Rebellion will be crushed.
It is the premature agitation of the Presidential question. When
the Rebellion broke out, I assumed that it would be put down in a
few months—for I assumed that this greatest crime against nationality and humanity would arouse and unite the whole North. How
greatly was I mistaken! Very soon the Democratic party was
seen to prefer itself to the country. The Republican party stood
by the country. But at the present time there is no little danger
that the country may be sacrificed in a strife between the members of the Republican party. For, taking advantage of this
strife, the Democratic party may succeed in getting the reins of
Government into the hands of one of its pro-slavery peacemakers.
But I may be asked—will not the rebels be conquered and the
country saved before the next Election? I still *hope* so—and until
the last few months I *believed* so. But is there not some reason
to fear that the North will be wrought up to a greater interest in
this year's Presidential than in this year's military campaign?
In other words, is there not some reason to fear that, for the
coming six months, politics instead of patriotism will be in the
ascendant?

I still say, as through the past winter I have frequently said,
written, and printed—that the Presidential question should not
have been talked of, no, nor so much as thought of, until midsummer. The first of September is quite early enough to make the
nomination; and in the mean time, undistracted by this so dis-
tracting subject, we should be working as one man for the one object of ending the Rebellion—and of ending it before reaching
the perils of a presidential election. And such working would
best educate us to make the best choice of a candidate. Moreover, it is the condition the country will be in three or four
months hence, rather than the condition it is now in, that should
be allowed to indicate the choice. Great and rapidly successive
are the changes in the circumstances of a country in time of war.
To nominate a President in time of peace, six months earlier than
is necessary, all would admit to be great folly. But greater folly
would it be to nominate him in time of war even a single month
earlier than is necessary. The Baltimore Convention is understood to be a movement for renominating President Lincoln, and
the Cleveland Convention one for nominating General Fremont.
Would that both Conventions were dropped! Would indeed
that the whole subject were dropped until July or August!—and
would too that it were dropped with the understanding, that it
should then be taken up, not by the politicians, but by the
people!

The people would present a loyal and an able candidate: and
whether it were Lincoln or Fremont, Chase or Butler, Dickinson
or Dix, the country would be safe.

I recall at this moment the large and respectable meeting for
consultation held in Albany last January. What a pity that the
meeting took fright at the temperate and timely resolutions re-

ported to it! What a pity that the meeting saw in them danger to the country, or perhaps, more properly speaking, to a party! One of these resolutions and its advocates urged the importance of postponing until the latest possible day the whole subject of a Presidential nomination : and, had it been adopted and published, it would not unlikely have exerted sufficient influence to bring about such postponement. Time has proved the wisdom of the other resolutions also. I wish I could, without seeming egotism, say that slavery, and slavery alone, having brought this war upon us, they, who have given but little thought to slavery, should be too modest to toss aside indignantly and sneeringly the suggestions of those who have made it their life-long study. Were these resolutions now published, almost every man who opposed them, would wonder that he had so little foresight as to oppose them.

And there is still another thing which should perhaps be allowed to suggest a doubt whether the rebellion will be crushed. It is, that we are so reluctant to pay the cost of crushing it. Our brave soldiers and sailors give their lives to this end. But we who stay at home shrink from the money tax which is, and which should be far more largely put upon us. Our nation is imperiled by the incessant outflow of a big stream of gold. Wise and patriotic as he is, our Secretary of the Treasury will nevertheless labor in vain to diminish this stream unless importations shall be taxed far more heavily. Deeply disgraceful are these importations when it is by all that is precious in the very life of our nation that they are forbidden. Surely it is no time now to be indulging in foreign luxuries : and as to necessaries, our own country can furnish them all. Luxuries, whether foreign or domestic, should all come now with great cost to the consumer. And only a small return for protecting their estates from the rebels would it be for the rich to pay over to Government one fourth, and the very rich one half of their incomes. Let me add in this connection that the State Banks should be so patriotic, as to rejoice in the national advantage of an exclusively National currency.

I expressed my belief that the rebellion will be crushed—but my doubt whether the nation will be saved. A guilty nation, like a guilty individual, can be saved through repentance only. But where are the proofs that this nation has so much as begun to repent of the great sin, which has brought the great calamity upon her? She has, it is true, done much to prove that she regards slavery as a political and economical evil, and a source of great peril to the nation : but she has done exceedingly little toward proving that she has a penitent sense of her sin in fastening the yoke of slavery on ten to twenty millions of this and former generations. It is only here and there—at wide intervals both of time and space—that has been heard the penitent exclamation, "We are verily guilty concerning our brother;"—only at these wide intervals that has been seen any relaxation of the national hatred and scorn for the black man. "Abolitionist," which, when the nation shall be saved, will be the most popular name in it, is still the most odious and contemptible name in it. That the fugitive slave statute is still suffered to exist, is ample proof that this nation has still a devil's heart toward the black man. How sad that even now, when because of the sin of slaveholding, God is making blood flow like water in this land, there should be found members of Congress, who claim this infernal statute to be one of the rights of slaveholding! As if slaveholding had rights! As if any thing else than punishment were due to it!—punishment adequate to its unmingled, unutterable, and blasphemous wrongs!

I shall, however, be told that slavery will soon be abolished by an Amendment of the Constitution. And what will such an Amendment say? Why, nothing more than that slavery ought not to be—must not be—when it shall no longer be constitutional. What, however, the American people need to say, is, that be it constitutional or unconstitutional, slavery shall not be. So they are always prepared to say regarding murder. But slavery is worse than murder. Every right-minded man had far rather his child were murdered than enslaved. Why, then, do they not affirm that, in no event, will they tolerate slavery any more than murder? The one answer is—because it is the black man, and the black man only, on whom slavery falls. Were white Americans to be enslaved in a Barbary State, or anywhere else, our nation would respect no pleadings of statutes or even of constitutions for their enslavement. In defiance of whatever pleas or whatever restraints, she would release them if she could. The most stupendous hypocrisy of which America has been guilty, is first professing that there is law for slavery—law for that which all law proclaims an outlaw—law for that in which there is not one element of law, but every element of which is an outrage upon law; and second, in professing it, not because she has a particle of belief in it—but simply because blacks instead of whites are the victims of her slavery. America declared that John Brown was "rightly hung." How hypocritical was the declaration, may be inferred from the fact that had they been white instead of black slaves whom he flung away his life to rescue, she would have honored him as perhaps man has never been honored. And she would have made his honors none the less, but heaped them up all the more, if, in prosecuting his heroic and merciful work, he had tossed aside statutes and broken through sacred constitutions. Oh! if this nation shall ever be truly saved, it will no longer regard John Brown as worthy of the fate of a felon; but it will build the whitest monuments to his memory, and cherish it as the memory of the sublimest and most Christlike man the nation has ever produced! Some of the judgments of John Brown—especially such as led him to Harper's Ferry—were unsound and visionary. Nevertheless, even when committing his mistakes, he stood, by force of the disinterestedness and greatness of his soul, above all his countrymen.

Would Congress contribute most effectively to put down the rebellion, and to save the nation by the great salvations of penitence and justice—the only real salvations? Would it do this?—then let it pass, solemnly and unanimously, a resolution that there never was and never can be, either inside or outside of statutes or constitutions, law for slavery; and then another resolution that whoever shall attempt to put the yoke of slavery on however humble a neck, black or white, deserves to be put to death.

A word further in regard to the proposed Amendment. Were the impudent and monstrous claim of its being law set up for murder, no one would propose an amendment of the Constitution forbidding murder. The only step in that case would be to make the penalty for the crime more sure and if possible more severe. Such an amendment would be strenuously objected to, in that it would stain the Constitution with the implication that murder had been constitutional. And now, if we shall have a Constitutional Amendment, which, in terms, forbids slavery, (it is already forbidden by the spirit, principles, and even provisions of the Constitution,) shall we not be virtually admitting to the world and to posterity that this nation had been guilty of tolerating, if not indeed of positively authorizing, in its Constitution the highest crime of earth? God save us from an admission, which shall serve both to stamp us with infamy and to perpetuate the infamy!

PETERBORO, April 26, 1864.

LETTER TO MRS. STANTON

ON THE PRESIDENTIAL QUESTION.

PETERBORO, June 6, 1864.

MRS. E. CADY STANTON, New-York :

MY DEAR COUSIN : I have your letter. It would be too great labor to answer all, who seek to know my choice amongst the presidential candidates. But I must answer *you*.

I have no choice. The first of September will be time enough for me and for every other person to have one. Intermediate events and changes will be indispensable lessons in our learning who should be the preferred candidate. To commit ourselves in time of war to a candidate one month before it is necessary, is worse than would be a whole year of such prematureness in time of peace. Then there is the absorbing, not to say frenzying, interest, which attends our important elections. That it is frenzying is manifest from the scornful reproach and wild invective, which the press is already heaping up on Lincoln and Fremont— both of them honest and able men, and both of them intent on saving the country. How unwise, nay how insane, to let this absorbing and frenzying interest come needlessly early into rivalry with our interest in the one great work of crushing the rebellion! For more than half a year have I frequently and faithfully, both with lips and pen, deprecated the premature agitation of the question who should be the chosen candidate. If, therefore, the Cleveland and Baltimore Conventions shall have the effect to divide the loyal voters so far as to let a pro-slavery and sham Democrat slip into the Presidency through their divisions, I, at least, shall not be responsible for the ruin that may come of it.

My concern whether it shall be Lincoln or Fremont or Chase or Butler or Grant who shall reach the presidential chair is comparatively very slight. But my concern to keep out of it a man, who would make any other terms with the rebels than their absolute submission is overwhelming. For any other terms would not only destroy our nation, but lessen the sacredness of nationality everywhere, and sadly damage the most precious interests of all mankind.

Since the Rebellion broke out, I have been nothing but an anti-rebellion man. So unconditionally have I gone for putting it down unconditionally, as to make no stipulations in behalf of my most cherished objects and dearest interests. And so shall I continue to go. I love the anti-slavery cause. Nevertheless, I would have the rebellion put down at whatever necessary expense to that cause. I love the Constitution; and deprecate the making of any even the slightest change in it. Nevertheless, I make infinitely less account of saving it than of destroying the rebellion. I love my country. But sooner than see her compromise with the rebels, I would see her exhaust herself and perish in her endeavors to defeat their crime—that greatest crime of all the ages and all the world. I do not forget that many of my old fellow abolitionists accuse me of having been unfaithful to the anti-slavery cause during the rebellion. My first answer to them is—that to help suppress the rebellion is the duty which stands nearest to me : and my second answer—that in no way so well as in suppressing it can the anti-slavery cause or any other good cause be promoted. There is not a good cause on the earth that has not an enemy in the unmixed and mighty wickedness of this rebellion.

You will rightly infer from what I have said, that my vote will be cast just where I shall judge it will be like to go farthest in keeping a disloyal man out of the Presidency. My definition of a disloyal man includes every one who would consent to obtain peace by concessions to the rebels — concessions however slight. Should the rebellion be disposed of before the election, I might possibly refuse to vote for any of the present candidates. When voting in time of war, and especially such a fearful war as the present, for a Governor or President, I vote for a leader in the war rather than for a civil ruler. Where circumstances leave me free to vote for a man with reference mainly to his qualifications as a civil ruler, I am, as my voting for thirty years proves, very particular how I vote. In 1856, Fremont was in nomination for the Chief Magistracy. I honored him—but I did not vote for him. In 1860, Lincoln was nominated for it. I had read his Debate with Senator Douglas, and I thought well of him. But neither for him did I vote. To-day, however, I could cheerfully vote for either to be the constitutional head of the army and navy. I go further, and say, that to save the Presidential office from going into the hands of one who would compromise with the rebels, I would vote for a candidate far more unsound on slavery than the severest abolition critic might judge either Lincoln or Fremont to be. But were there no such danger, I would sternly refuse to vote for any man who recognizes, either in or out of the Constitution, a law for slavery, or who would graduate any human rights, natural or political, by the color of the skin.

This disposition to meddle with things before their time is one that has manifested itself, and worked badly, all the way through the war. The wretched attempts at "Reconstruction" are an in-

stance of it. "Reconstruction" should not so much as have been
spoken of before the rebellion was subdued. I hope that by
that time all loyal men, the various doctrines and crotchets to the
contrary notwithstanding, will be able to see that the seceded
States did, practically as well as theoretically, get themselves out
of the Union and Nation—as effectually out as if they had never
been in. Our war with Mexico ended in a treaty of peace with
her. Doubtless our war with the South will end in like manner.
If we are the conqueror, the treaty will, I assume, be based on
the unconditional surrender of the South. And then the South,
having again become a portion of our nation, Congress will be
left as free to ordain the political divisions of her territory, as it
was to ordain those of the territory we conquered from Mexico.
Next in order, Congress will very soon, as I have little doubt, see
it to be safe and wise to revive our old State lines. Nevertheless,
I trust, that such revival would never be allowed until Congress
should see it to be clearly safe and wise. We hear much of the
remaining constitutional rights of the loyal men in the seceded
States. But they, no more than their rebellious neighbors, have
such rights. It is true that the rebellion is their misfortune
instead of their crime. Nevertheless, it severed every political
cord as well between the nation and themselves as between the
nation and those rebellious neighbors. The seceded States embarked in a revolution, which swept away all the political relations of all their people, loyal as well as disloyal. Such is the
hazard, which no man, however good, can escape from. If the
major part or supreme power of his State carries it to destruction,
he is carried along with it. A vigilant, informed, active, influential member of his body politic does it therefore behoove every
good man to be.

In his haste for "Reconstruction," the President went forward
in it—whereas he is entitled to not the least part in it, until Congress has first acted in it. In the setting up of military or provisional governments, as we proceed in our conquests, his is the
controlling voice — for he is the military head of the nation.
But in regard to the setting up of civil governments in the wake
of those conquests, he is entitled to no voice at all until after Congress has spoken.

Another instance of meddling with things before their time is
this slapping of the face of France with the "Monroe Doctrine."
I was about to say that doing so serves but to provoke the enmity
of France. There is, however, one thing more which it provokes—
and that is the ridicule of the world. For us, whilst the rebels
are still at the throat of our nation, and may even be at her
funeral, to be resolving that we will protect the whole Western
Continent from the designs of the whole Eastern Continent, is
as ludicrous a piece of impotent bravado as ever the world
laughed at.

And still another instance of our foolish prematureness is the
big words in which we threaten to punish the leaders of the

rebellion. It would be time enough for these big words when
we had subdued the rebellion and captured the leaders. In the
mean time there should be only big blows. Moreover, if we shall
succeed in getting these leaders into our hands, it will be a question for the gravest consideration whether we should not beg
their pardon instead of punishing them. What was it that
stirred up the rebellion? The spirit of slavery. That alone is
the spirit by means of which Southern treason can build up a fire
in the Southern heart whose flames shall burst out in rebellion.
Slavery gone from the South, and there will never more be rebellions there to disturb the peace and prosperity in which North
and South will ever after dwell together. Which was the guiltier
party in feeding and inflaming that spirit? The pro-slavery and
preponderant North. The guiltier North it was, that had the
more responsible part in moulding the leaders of the rebellion.
Does it then become this guiltier North to be vengeful toward
these her own creations—her own children?—and, what is more,
vengeful toward them for the bad spirit which she herself had so
large a share in breathing into them?—for the Satanic character
which she herself did so much to produce in them? But I shall
be told that the North has repented of her part in upholding
slavery, and thereby furnishing the cause of the rebellion; and
that the South should have followed her example. But if her
repentance did not come until after the rebellion broke out, then
surely it came too late to save her from responsibility for the
rebellion. Has it, however, come even yet? I see no proof of
it. I can see none so long as the American people continue to
trample upon the black man. God can see none. Nor will he
stay his desolating judgments so long as the American Congress,
instead of wiping out penitently and indignantly all fugitive slave
statutes, is infatuated enough to be still talking of "the rights
of slaveholders," and of this being "a nation for white men."
Assured let us be, that God will never cease from his controversy
with this guilty nation until it shall have ceased from its base
and blasphemous policy of proscribing, degrading, and outraging
portions of his one family. The insult to him in the persons of
his red and black children, of which Congress was guilty in its
ordinance for the Territory of Montana, will yet be punished in
blood, if it be not previously washed out in the tears of penitence. And this insult, too, whilst the nation is under God's
blows for like insults! What a silly as well as wicked Congress!
And then that such a Congress should continue the policy of providing chaplains for the army! Perhaps, however, it might be
regarded as particularly fit for such a Congress to do this. Chaplains to pray for our country's success whilst our country continues to perpetrate the most flagrant and diabolical forms of injustice! As if the doing of justice were not the indispensable way
of praying to the God of Justice! It is idle to imagine that God
is on the side of this nation. He can not be with us. For whilst
he is everywhere with justice, he is nowhere with injustice. I

2

admit that he is not on the side of the rebellion. From nothing
in all his universe can his soul be further removed than from this
most abominable of all abominations. If we succeed in putting
it down, our success, so far as God is concerned, will be only
because he hates the rebellion even more than he hates our
wickedness. To expect help from him in any other point of view
than this, is absurd. Aside from this, our sole reliance must be,
as was the elder Napoleon's, on having "the strongest battal-
ions." I believe we shall succeed—but that it will be only for the
reasons I have mentioned—only because we are the stronger party
and that God is even more against the rebels than he is against
us. How needful, however, that we guard ourselves from con-
founding success against the rebellion with the salvation of the
nation! Whether the nation shall be saved is another question
than whether the rebellion shall be suppressed. In the providence of God, even a very wicked nation may be allowed to
become a conqueror—may be used to punish another wicked
nation before the coming of its own turn to be conquered and
punished. But a nation, like an individual, can be saved only by
penitence and justice.

LETTER TO MESSRS. WADE AND DAVIS.

PETERBORO, August 8, 1864.

HON. B. F. WADE,
HON. H. WINTER DAVIS:

GENTLEMEN: I have read your Protest. It is a strongly reasoned and instructive paper. Nevertheless, I regret its appearance. For it will serve to reduce the public good-will towards Mr. Lincoln; and that is what, just at this time, the public interest can not afford. It may turn out that Mr. Lincoln is the man for whom it will be vital to the national existence to cast the largest possible vote. Personally he may not be more worthy of it than Mr. Fremont or Mr. Chase, or some other man, who may be nominated. But, if as the election draws near, it shall be seen that he will probably get a larger vote than any other candidate of the uncompromising opponents of the rebellion, then it will be the absolute duty of every one of them to vote for him. The election of a man who would consent to any thing short of the unconditional surrender of those, who, without even the slightest cause of complaint, have made war upon us, would not only be the ruin of our nation, but it would be also the base betrayal of that sacred cause of nationality, which they of one nation owe it to those of every other nation, the earth over, to cherish and maintain. But no such consequence, nor any other fatal consequence, would there be, should a loyal man of whatever faults be elected—a man who, because he is loyal, would in no event fail to insist on the absolute submission of those who had causelessly rebelled against their country. Hence, though it may be at the expense of passing by our favorite candidate, we should nevertheless all feel ourselves urged by the strongest possible motives to cast our votes just where they will be like to contribute most to defeat the compromising or sham peace candidate.

Mr. Lincoln, although an able, honest, patriotic man, has fallen into grave errors. But who, in his perplexing circumstances, would have been exempt from them? He has depended too largely on the policy of conciliation. He has made too much account of pleasing Border States and Peace Democrats. But in all this he has sought not his own advantage, but the safety of his coun try from the harm with which Border States and Peace Democrats (same thing as Pro-Slavery Democrats) threatened her.

Nor has Mr. Lincoln always kept himself within the sphere of his office. I do not mean that he went out of it in imprisoning a few treasonable men. He should have imprisoned more. Nor do I refer to his suppression of a few treasonable newspapers. He should have suppressed many more. In almost any other nation with rebels at its throat, the printing of "the forged Proclamation" would have been visited with the severest penalties. The plea that the offense was committed where war was not actual, would have been scouted. Nay, the presumption to offer it would have been lacking. By the way, the city of New-York is emphatically a theater of the war. Thousands there with worse than Southern hearts—for Northern rebels are worse than Southern rebels—are constantly plotting war against their country. Occasionally their war comes to the surface. It did so when, a little more than a year ago, it broke out in plunders and murders meaner and more malignant than the world had ever before seen. It will break out again as soon as some other conjunction of circumstances shall promise success. New-York not a theater of the war! Why, we have immeasurably more to fear from the ever-warring disloyalty of New-York and Philadelphia, than from the swords and guns of Richmond and Atlanta. But what if there be not actual war, has been none, and will probably be none in the locality where the press utters treason?—may not the war power lay its suppressing hand on that press? If it may not, then the country may be lost. For, in the first place, civil proceedings may be too slow to save it; and, in the second place, the locality may be too disloyal to favor even civil proceedings. New-York has not favored them. She has not punished her treasonable newspapers; and that she has not is strong proof that she will not, and is of itself ample reason why the war power should. Moreover, however loyal might be the locality, it would not be right in all cases for the war power to depend upon her motions. In a matter, which is vital to the nation, the nation itself must act. Her life must not be left to hinge upon the will or conduct of any locality, however loyal.

I have virtually said that a treasonable press is capable of working ruin to a country. "The forged Proclamation," for instance, was a blow at the credit and at the very life of the nation. But for the intervention of the military arm it would have done much evil, and other disloyal presses would have been emboldened to do more. I add that if it were left alone to the civil authority to watch the presses in the North, a very considerable share of them would quickly be teeming with treason. If, then, the war power is as limited as last Saturday's Opinion of the Court in the case of The People *against* General Dix makes it, and if also that power shall submit to that limitation, then of necessity will the work of debauching the Northern mind by a disloyal Northern press go on toward its fatal result even more rapidly than ever.

The jurisdiction of General Dix is called in question. It is as ample and absolute as that of Sherman before Atlanta or Grant before Richmond. Were citizens of New-York to strike Government troops in that city, he clearly would have as much right to strike back as have Sherman and Grant in such a case; and as clearly he would no more than they be under obligation to wait for redress at the hands of the civil authorities. But the right of the military commander to strike back, when newspapers strike at the existence of the nation, is even more vital. A single column of newspaper treason might imperil the nation more than could many columns of armed foes. Is it said that so great power in an individual is very dangerous? I grant it. And therefore we must as far as possible keep out of war — for in war there must be such power in a single hand.

I do not fear that General Dix will abuse his office. He is both a wise and a just man: and that he, who has borne himself so beautifully in our war, should be degraded to a culprit in our courts— and this too in return for a service he did his country—makes us blush for that country. It was he who in his Order, at the very beginning of the War, *to shoot down the man who should strike down the flag*, sounded the very key-note of that patriotic spirit in which it was our duty to conduct the War. In that Order he virtually bade us all stand *unconditionally* by our country against whatever rebels or rascals.

I honor the good intentions of President Lincoln. But I would that he had the nerve to meet, as General Jackson would have met, these traitorous men amongst us, who, when the state of the country is such as to make its salvation turn on a liberal interpretation of the powers of the Executive, study the reduction and belittling of those powers. Valuable as are the virtues of forbearance and forgiveness, we have had quite too much of them for our safety. Stern justice, whilst always a no less excellent virtue, is, in the time of stern war, a far more timely and necessary one. Would that the President might mingle a little more of it with his kind and patient spirit!

I said that the President has not always kept himself within his official limits. His Amnesty Proclamation is one of the instances in which he has exceeded them. In his military capacity he had nothing to do with the reconstruction of civil governments; and in no other capacity had he any thing to do with it until Congress had acted upon it. It was for him to set up military governments in the wake of our advancing armies. But it was not for him to concern himself about the permanent or civil governments, that would come to take the place of these temporary provisions.

By many the President is condemned for his slowness. Perhaps he is too slow in some things. There are others, however, in which he is too fast. But in this latter fault the great mass of the loyal men both in and out of Congress are with him. I agree with you that the President's plan of settlement is a wrong one.

But your Congressional plan, like his, is premature. How much precious time was wasted over the premature question of the confiscation of real estate! Not a foot of it should have been sold before the close of the war. Nothing should have been done with it but to lease the vacant portions of it—and that only from year to year. No great inconvenience could ensue from such a postponement of the sale of Southern soil, nor from such a postponement of the setting up of civil government upon it. War and especially such a war as this — is no time for unnecessary work. It will not be well done. Moreover, the doing of it will leave necessary work ill-done.

Then there is the unseasonable work of altering the Constitution. Not one moment should have been wasted in that worse than useless direction. If nothing in the Constitution hinders the most effectual prosecution of the war, then surely there is no excuse for embarrassing ourselves in time of war with attempts to alter it. If, on the other hand, any thing in it stands in the way of such prosecution, Congress can virtually overcome it. For the Constitution does itself accord to Congress the power to make whatever laws it thinks "necessary and proper" for carrying on the war, be it even laws for taking into military service every slave and every apprentice or every schoolhouse and every church in the land. A nation is no nation—certainly it could not long be one—that does not recognize such absolute power.

Then there is the undue haste to come to the terms of peace—a haste with which the President is no more chargeable than thousands of loyal men. When they who without the least provocation took up arms to dismember our beloved country, shall lay them down, then and not till then are we to be for peace, or for any thing but war. Then and not till then, are we to talk or even to think of the terms of peace. The war ended, and then will be the time for our concessions to our deluded brethren. Just and generous may these concessions be! There are many good people who, in their great desire for peace, would have the war ended on any terms. They would even come to the ever-insisted-on terms of the rebels, and accept of disunion. But these good people are foolish people. There can be no peace in disunion. A truce, and a very brief one, is the best there could be. War would break out every few years. Besides that we can get a peace only by conquering it, it can abide only on the condition of reünion.

And then these premature Presidential nominations, which for six months I was so earnestly deprecating. God grant that they may not fatally divide us! God grant that they may not fatally divert our interest from the prosecution of the war! But the blame of these nominations rests not on the President, but on the mass of his party.

The putting down of the rebellion—that is our one present work. Our absorption in it should be so entire, as to leave us no time and no heart for any thing which is unnecessary, or for any thing which is necessary until the very day, nay the very hour, when it has become necessary.

I scarcely need add that in giving ourselves to the work of overthrowing the rebellion we are to make no conditions. I scarcely need add that those Democrats are to be condemned, who insist-on stipulating for the safety of slavery ere they can embark in this work ; nor that those abolitionists are also to be condemned who put the abolition of slavery before the suppression of the rebellion. This suppression is the duty which must be discharged, come what will of its discharge to the Democratic or the abolition party. For it is the nearest duty. Moreover, let the abolitionist magnify the crime of slavery as he will, the crime of the rebellion remains the far greater one. For the rebellion superadds to all that is bad in slavery, parricidal blows at the life of the country and contempt of the sacredness of nationality. I have myself been a somewhat earnest advocate of abolition. But at no time during the rebellion have I felt at liberty to inquire of abolition whether, or how, I should work toward putting down the rebellion. I add that, as the sole legitimate object of the war we are prosecuting is to put down the rebellion, therefore none have the right to embarrass or pervert the war by their schemes to harm or their schemes to help slavery. We do not say that the abolitionist is to cease working against or the anti-abolitionist is to cease working for slavery. But we do say that the putting down of the rebellion is the common work of abolitionists and anti-abolitionists, Democrats and Republicans : and that, differ as they may in other respects, they are to be one in the prosecution of this common work. A traitor to his country is he who, when traitors have fallen upon her, allows himself under the counsels of any party, however dear, any interest, however cherished, or any cause, however sacred, to withhold his help from her. Such party, such interest, such cause notwithstanding, he is to be " arm and soul " against the traitors.

I repeat that I regret your Protest—or rather, I should say, the unseasonable publication of it. There is a great deal of truth in it—and generally a very forcible presentation of that truth. But the country can not now afford to have the hold of Mr. Lincoln on the popular confidence weakened. Pardon me for saying that the eve of the Presidential Election is not the time to be making an issue with Mr. Lincoln in regard to either his real or supposed errors. For, from present indications, it is highly probable that we shall need to concentrate upon him the votes of all the loyal voters in order to defeat the disloyal candidate. Issues with the Southern rebels and their Northern friends are the only ones we can afford to make before the election. Let Lincoln get all the loyal votes, let Fremont get them, let Chase get them, let any other loyal man get them, if this shall be necessary to prevent the election of one who is in the interest of the rebellion and of a spurious peace. I doubt not from your ardent patriotism and your strong sense, that you entirely agree with me at this point ; and

that they altogether misjudge you, who suppose that you will in no
event vote for Mr. Lincoln. The election of no loyal man, however faulty he may be, can destroy the nation. But the election
of whatever disloyal man will. Strong as is your dislike of some
of Mr. Lincoln's measures, you will not suffer it to stand in the
way of your voting to save the country, nor in the way of your
entreating others to do so.

ON McCLELLAN'S NOMINATION AND ACCEPTANCE.

I WRITE these pages for the candid. Partisans would not hear me. They follow party. Those only will hear me who follow truth; and who will still follow it at whatever expense to party. The North is divided — fearfully divided. One portion holds that the North, and the other that the South is the guilty party in this war. Which of them is right, is the great, nay the only question to be answered at the coming Election. If the North is the guilty party, then McClellan should be preferred. If the South, then Lincoln. I name them because every day makes it more evident that all our votes will finally be concentrated on them. McClellan is the candidate of those who hold the North to be the guilty party, and therefore whatever exceptions some of them take to him, all will feel constrained to vote for him. So, too, all who hold that the South is the guilty party, will feel it to be their duty to vote for Lincoln. Many of them would prefer to vote for Fremont, if they could thereby vote as effectively to defeat the candidate whose sympathies are with the South. But this they now see they can not do. It is in this wise that Fremont and Cochrane will themselves, notwithstanding their dislike of some of his measures, vote for Lincoln. They are too magnanimous to let personal considerations hinder them from voting for him; and they are too patriotic to withhold a vote, which they think the salvation of the country calls for. Nay, they will hasten to inspire their friends with the like magnanimity and patriotism. So, too, the great influence of Wendell Phillips will be brought to the side of Lincoln, as soon as he shall see that the man to be elected must be either Lincoln or a servant of the South. Strong as is his preference for Fremont, he will not let it work to the destruction of his country.

We need not go back of the Convention, which nominated Lincoln, to learn that the Union party lays all the blame of the war upon the South. Nor need we go back of the Convention, which nominated McClellan, to learn that the Democratic party lays all the blame of it on the North. The proceedings of the Chicago Convention afford conclusive evidence that the Democratic party is identified with the rebellion; is at peace with the enemies in-

stead of the friends of the nation—at peace with the South, and
at war with the North, Nevertheless, it is not to be condemned,
but rather to be honored for this, provided the North is the guilty
party in the war. I am not of those whose motto is: "Our
country, right or wrong." It is only when she is right, that I am
with her. I can be loyal to the North so far only as she is loyal
to justice. Nor, if I would, could I help her wherein she breaks
with justice. A nation, like an individual, puts herself beyond
the reach of help in proportion as she defies the claims of truth
and righteousness.

Let me here say that McClellan, no more than any other member of the Democratic party, is necessarily worthy of condemnation for opposing the cause in which his country is embarked.
Nay, if it is an unrighteous cause, then it is proper in him to
stand forth against it—to stand forth as distinctly and emphatically as he does by accepting his nomination at the hands of the
enemies of that cause.

I repeat, the question to be passed upon at the coming election
is — which is the guilty party in this war—the North or the
South? It is admitted that the South took up arms to dismember
our nation: and that she robbed it of moneys, forts, guns, and
portions of our little standing army. It is admitted, too, that it
was only in reply to these outrages, that we armed ourselves.
Hence whilst the war on her part is offensive, on ours it is but
defensive. Notwithstanding all this, the North may not be the
innocent party. For she may have oppressed and provoked the
South beyond endurance. I am slow to admit that any rebellion
in a land where there is free access to the ballot-box can be justified. Nevertheless, if it can be shown that it was because she
was made to suffer intolerable oppressions that she flew to
arms, I will not condemn her. Had she such oppressions to
complain of ?

It is said, more in Europe, however, than in America, that our
high tariff was a burden upon the South. Never, however, had
we a tariff so nearly approaching free-trade, as when her States
began to secede. Moreover, the South could have had it as much
lower as she pleased. What, however, if our tariff were not a
proper one ?— that surely would not be enough to justify rebellion.

Had the South any right to call herself oppressed by the election of Lincoln ? None at all. He was elected constitutionally.
But he was against slavery ! It is true that he was—only mod-
erately so, however. Several of the Presidents immediately pre-
ceding him were thoroughly *for* slavery. And yet the North did
not claim that she was oppressed by their election. Least of all,
did she claim that their election furnished ground for rebellion.

Was the South at liberty to regard herself oppressed because
so much was said at the North against slavery ? Certainly not.
The Constitution provides for free speech. Moreover, the South
spoke as freely against our systems of labor, as we did against

her slavery. She sneered at our "small-fisted farmers" and our "greasy mechanics." She stigmatized our noble laborers as "the mudsills of society." Then, too, the South helps send missionaries over the earth to argue against idolatries and other abominations; and thus is she estopped by her own acts from forbidding others to search and criticise herself.

Was the South oppressed by Northern legislation against slavery? Never. The North was always willing to have the Supreme Court of the United States pass upon such legislation. When, however, the North sent Commissioners to the South, to induce her to consent to have the constitutionality of those laws under which she was casting Northern freemen into the pit of slavery, passed upon by that Court, those Commissioners had to fly for their lives before the murderous onset made upon them.

But John Brown, and at other times, other Northern men, went into the Southern States to help persons escape from slavery! The North, however, was not responsible for this. She ever stood by slavery, and helped the South tighten the chains of the slaves. Little right has the South to complain of the sympathy of John Brown and others with her slaves. Where these delivered one slave, her kidnappers made slaves of ten Northern freemen. But there was rejoicing at the North over the escape of Southern slaves! I admit it. So was there rejoicing at the South over the escape of Southern men from Algerine slavery. Such rejoicings can not be stopped. And all attempts of the South to stop them, will be vain attempts to change human nature.

Was the South oppressed by the refusal of the Northern people to accede to a proposition of the Southern people to have an amicable separation of the States, and an amicable division of the territories, and other national property? There was no proposition from the Southern people to the Northern people. There was a proposition from Southern individuals, unauthorized by the Southern people; and it was made not to our people, but to our Government— to a Government which, instead of being authorized to dismember our nation, is sworn to preserve it, and which, instead of being authorized to throw away the Constitution, is sworn to keep it sacred and unbroken. The people of the North were ready to meet the people of the South in a Convention of Delegates. They were ready to make large concessions, in order to save from disruption the nation so dear to them. Entirely ready they were, I am sorry to believe, to indorse and consummate the remarkable action of Congress in favor of altering the Constitution to the advantage of slavery. In fine, they would have consented to almost any demand of the South short of the sundering of the nation. This they would not consent to: and, because she knew they would not, the South would not have the National Convention. The sundering of the nation was the one thing she was intent on; and nothing else, nor all things else, would she accept in lieu of it. Hence to get this one thing,

which she could not hope to get otherwise, she resorted to arms.
Herein and herein only, is the explanation of the outbreak of the
rebellion. Could she but have been brought to recede-from her
determination to set up a nation for herself and by herself, all
other difficulties with the South might have been adjusted. It is
in no degree necessary to my argument, to explain why she then
insisted, has ever since insisted, and never more strenuously than
now, on this national independence. Nevertheless, as some, under
whose eye this paper may fall, might like to meet with the explanation, I will give it. The whole explanation of this pertinacity
on the part of the South, is to be found in the fact that she is
determined to maintain slavery, and that she despairs of maintaining it, unless she shall erect herself into a nation, independent
of every other nation. The South saw slavery cast out of all
Europe, and all American slavery except her own to be tottering.
She saw too, that the North was every day becoming more enlightened in regard to slavery, and therefore more hostile to it.
Hence the great and absorbing question with her was—what she
should do most effectually to insulate herself, and shut out those
ever-swelling floods of anti-slavery sentiment, and anti-slavery
influence, which were constantly pouring in upon her. Her natural decision was to build up about herself the high and, as she
hoped, impervious walls of a new nationality. The North she
regarded as already abolitionized. To remain, therefore, in connection with her, was to allow herself, also, to be abolitionized.
Hence she broke off from the North. For what else would she
have consented to break off from it, and to lose the incalculable
advantage of being a part of this great nation?

In all this, which I have now referred to, and I know not that
there is any thing more of this bearing to refer to, has the South
suffered intolerable oppressions? Nay, has she suffered any oppression? None whatever. In our national affairs, she was generally allowed to have her own way. I admit that we wronged
her: but never, even in the slightest degree, did we oppress her.
And the only way in which she was ever wronged by us, was our
shameful indulgence of both her tyrannous spirit, and her greed
of place and power. Surely, surely, then, the North is not to be
accused of provoking the rebellion. Surely, surely, then, the
South is the guilty, and the only guilty party in the rebellion.
And surely, surely, then, the North can not, without making herself very criminal, and very base, vote for the candidate of those,
who hold the North, and not the South, to be the guilty party.
But it may be said that their candidate (General McClellan) does
not hold in this respect, as they do who nominated him. If he
does not, then is he very unfortunate in being misrepresented by
his friends, who put him forth as the representative of themselves,
and who, it is fair to suppose, knew him thoroughly when they
did so. Since the Northern men, who espouse the cause of the
South, single out McClellan for their standard-bearer, it would be
madness in us, who cleave to the cause of the North, to believe

him to be with us and to vote for him. If he is indeed a North-
side man, nevertheless, since they, who know him, have set him
forth as a South-side one, he can not complain of us for not voting
for him. He can complain but of his friends, who have misrepresented him, and whose misrepresentations justify us in withholding our votes from him. But we are cited to McClellan's letter
of acceptance. That it is a letter of *acceptance* is of itself sufficient to disentitle him to the vote of every loyal man. That he
is the candidate of a Convention composed of the open enemies
of that cause for which his country is pouring out her treasure
and her blood—composed of those whose war is upon the North
only—is surely reason enough why no intelligent friend of that
cause can give him his vote. But we will look further into this
letter. I said that the North is divided between those who hold
the North, and those who hold the South to be the guilty party.
On which side does McClellan's letter place him? It spares the
South, but it abounds in inculpations of the North. The indirect
and unmanly way in which he makes, or rather insinuates his
charges against the Government, was doubtless intended to render them more effective. It will, however, serve but to denote
the lack of an open, brave, and manly spirit in their author. He
has nothing to say of the barbarity with which the South con-
ducts the war—murdering fresh captives—or, if sparing them,
sparing thousands to be tortured in spirit and body, thousands
to be starved to death, and (worst fate of all!) thousands to be
sunk in slavery. Nothing of all this does he say. But, in his
characteristic, cowardly, roundabout way, he accuses the North
of the high crime of perverting the war. I grant that there have
been a few instances in which anti-slavery zealots have shown
their disposition to pervert it, and innumerable instances in which
pro-slavery zealots have shown the like. Just here let me say,
that miserable men are all they who, when monsters are striking
parricidal blows at the country, are incapable of making a single
and square issue with those monsters, and are intent on mixing
up with the one question of putting down these monsters conditions in behalf of or against Slavery, *Habeas Corpus*, or something
else. "Down with the rebellion, come what will of it to any of
our schemes, or theories, or interests," is the voice of wisdom.
Moreover, if slavery or anti-slavery, this or that political party,
this or that church, shall be found to stand in the way of putting
it down, let them all be swept out of the way. Nothing is worth
preserving, that stands in the way of putting down so unmitigated and unparalleled a wickedness as the rebellion. When it
shall have been put down, will be time to decide (and not till
then will it be time so much as to consider it) whether the safety
of the nation shall call for the weakening or strengthening of
slavery, for its utter annihilation, or for overspreading the whole
land with it. In the mean time, use slavery, or apprenticeship,
or any thing else in whatever way you can use it most effectually
to the crushing of the rebellion: and let all heads, all hearts,

and all hands find their one thought, one feeling, and one work to that end.

I admitted that there were instances of a disposition to pervert the war. But by far the most signal of all the instances of the actual perverting of the war, and of perverting it even to the direct help of the rebels, is that of McClellan himself. He it was, who began his mediating military career—his half-one-way and half-the-other way generalship—with a proclamation of safety to the foe at that very point where the foe was most vulnerable and most alarmed. He it was, who assured the slaveholders, that he would guard their homes, their wives and children, from servile insurrection, and who thereby left them free to go forth to swell rebellion's battling hosts. And now for him whose duty, instead of ministering peace and security to the enemy, was to leave him appalled and paralyzed with every possible terror—and now for him, I say, to throw out in his cowardly way his utterly false charge that the Government has perverted the war, is enough to make the soul of every honest man boil over with indignation. Very far am I from saying that McClellan should have favored servile insurrection. But I do say that he should have left the slaveholders to all their fears from their slaves, and to all that occupation of their thoughts and time which those fears called for. I add that his relieving them of those fears and of that occupation, was treason to his country—was even literal treason—for it was "adhering to her enemies, giving them aid and comfort."

McClellan professes great love of the Constitution and the Union. I love them. The costliest gift whereby I might contribute to preserve them I have not withheld. Both in peace, and in war, abundantly with both lips and pen, I have opposed even the slightest alteration in the Constitution. But whilst McClellan sees our Government making war upon the Union and the Constitution, I see no other war upon them than that which his own party and its Southern allies are waging.

I said that I love the Constitution. But I love my country more. I would use the Constitution to save the country. But the Democrats juggle with it to destroy the country. Instance their incessant knavish talk about the constitutional rights and the reserved rights of the seceded States. Whereas the plain fact is, that those States did, in seceding, forfeit every right but the right to be punished. France, were England to conquer her, would have no *right* to the present political subdivisions of her soil: and the South, being a rebel, and the guiltiest of all rebels, will, if conquered, be more emphatically destitute of all *right* to hers. I would hope that her old State lines might be recognized: but this would be for her conqueror alone to determine. The theory so industriously and injuriously and traitorously inculcated by the Democrats—that what were rights before the rebellion, must be rights after it, ay, and all the way through it—is the veriest nonsense. I have instanced the talk of the Democrats at one point. Instance, too, their incessant knavish talk about carrying on the war according to the Constitution. They know that the nation, which should try to carry on war according to a Constitution, would certainly perish: and hence, indeed is it that they are continually urging the Administration to make this altogether unprecedented experiment. Our Constitution does not attempt the folly of prescribing the way in which we shall carry on war. The simple truth in this matter, (and they are either silly or disingenuous who deny it,) is that war must ever be a law unto itself, and that no other law can meet its exigencies.

I said that I love the Union. My whole heart is set on its restoration: and therefore have I done all I could to *compel* the South to return to it. I say *compel*, because I believe she must be *compelled*. During all the years of the rebellion McClellan and his party have constantly held that the South would return to the Union, if the North would prepare the way. But the South has as constantly held to 'the contrary. For the reasons I have already given, the South will not consent to return. She has set up her new nation with slavery for its boasted corner-stone; and she will not, but upon compulsion, belong again to a nation of another kind. There is, I admit, one way in which the South might possibly be induced to return to the Union. That way McClellan and his party know; and that way I have not the slightest doubt they are willing, and no small share of them eager, to prepare. Should the North consent to set up slavery within all her borders and to put, as slavery requires, the claim of property in man on the same footing with the claim of property in horses and hogs, the South might possibly consent to return to the Union. The Democratic party knows that this is the only way in which she would consent to return, and this way the Democratic party would open to her.

The pernicious cry that our sole legitimate object in prosecuting the war is to save the Constitution and the Union, is, of course, abundantly echoed in McClellan's letter. The declarations both in and out of Congress in the early stages of the war that our one work was to restore the Constitution and the Union, I am not disposed to criticise. But very unwise was it to repeat such declarations, after the rebellion had taken on its wide dimensions, and was putting forth its gigantic and appalling efforts. Then our one work was to put down the rebellion; and, if need be, at whatever expense to Constitution or Union. The forms of the Constitution and the terms of the Union had then become of comparatively little account. Nay, the rebellion, greatest of all the crimes earth ever knew, must go down, though all do go down with it. Alas! how unreasonable and insane for the enemies of the rebellion at such a time as this, when the common work of putting it down claims the hands of all, and all the interest of all, to be making issues between themselves about the character of the Constitution, or the conditions of the Union! Put down the rebellion! Put it down now, and unconditionally! Matters about the Constitution and the Union can be adjusted afterward. This Democratic shouting for the Constitution and the Union, is but to call us off from crushing the rebellion.

I notice McClellan's pathetic appeal for the votes of the soldiers and sailors. What an impudent affectation in him to profess regard for these brave and devoted men, whilst he worms his way up to the platform, in which the cause they are battling, bleeding, and dying for, is condemned, and its abandonment called for! I say its *abandonment*—for such is the only possible meaning of the immediate armistice or " cessation of hostilities," which the platform demands. If, as President Lincoln's favorite story says, it is "no time to swap horses when crossing the stream," so it is no time to stop horses when crossing it. To stop at that critical moment is to expose all to go down-stream. For us to stop the war at this time, is to abandon the war, and to make vain all we have sacrificed in prosecuting it. Moreover, it is to abandon it when we are on the very eve of accomplishing its one object—the overthrow of the rebellion. I said it was an impudent affectation in McClellan, whilst indorsing the platform which insults the brave men who are fighting our battles, to be professing regard for them. So is it for him to be professing that regard whilst he places himself on that platform by the side of a Vice-Presidential candidate, whose sympathies with the South are as open as his own are sly! This candidate, for whom also is necessarily every vote cast for McClellan, and who, if elected, becomes in no very improbable event, the President of the United States, is the George H. Pendleton, who is a member of Congress, and who in that capacity steadily votes against supplies of men and moneys and taxes for carrying on the war. He is the same Pendleton, who with but nineteen others voted against censuring Harris for using treasonable language on the floor of Congress, and who with but fifteen others voted against the resolution, which declares the duty of crushing the rebellion. Greatly mistaken is McClellan if, with his unenviable military reputation and his base and guilty political connections, he hopes to catch our discerning soldiers and sailors with such chaff as his heartless praises of them. They read him " like a book." They will turn their backs upon him; and will give their approving faces and their approving votes to the honest Lincoln, who deals in no twattle about the Constitution and Union, and who speaks what he means; to the patriotic and earnest Lincoln, who believes in the cause for which our soldiers and sailors are contending, who does his utmost to reinforce them, and who scouts as spurious any peace with the rebels, which shall precede their unconditional surrender. This attempt of McClellan to get the votes of the armed defenders of the country, reminds us of the similar attempt of the Convention that nominated him. In one of its resolutions, the Democratic party is made to promise to take " care " of " the soldiery." Impudent and insulting promise! Undoubtedly " the soldiery " will, in turn, take care of the Democratic party. It will take care of it at the approaching election : and when the war is over at the South, and the day of reckoning for Northern rascality shall have come, it will again take care of the Northern traitors whose sympathies have made strong the hands of Southern traitors, and who have in this wise greatly prolonged the war, and greatly swollen the sum of the sufferings of our army.

I spoke of McClellan's worming his way up to the platform, which the Convention prepared for him and his fellow peace man to stand on. He did not mount it like a bad bold man, but crawled upon it like a bad timid one. His timidity, however, was in no wise because of a disagreement between the platform and his own views—for he virtually says that there is no disagreement between them when he says : "Believing that the views here expressed are those of the Convention and the people you represent, I accept the nomination." He believes that the Convention and its constituents agree with him for the sufficient reason that, having read their platform, he finds himself agreeing with them. It is well that the traitorous and infamous platform is so outspoken, since in this wise, inasmuch as McClellan does himself believe that he and its framers mean the same thing, we are enabled to put confident interpretations upon the double-meaning phraseologies in his cunning and cowardly letter. Oh no! McClellan's shyness of the platform was in no degree because he dissented from it—for he did not dissent from it. It was solely because he feared that his open, plump indorsement of a peace platform would leave him no votes but those of the Peace Democrats.

I have not failed to notice the patriotic, brave, and warlike words with which McClellan has sprinkled his letter. Inasmuch, however, as they are at entire variance with other parts of it and with the obvious spirit and aim of the whole ; and inasmuch, also, as they are repugnant to both the entire body and soul of that platform which by his acceptance of his nomination, as well as otherwise, he expresses his approval of; and inasmuch, moreover, as these cunningly flung-in words are out of all harmony with the words and deeds of that other George who stands beside him, and of the unprincipled party which nominated them—inasmuch as all this is so, I make no account of them. I cast the affected words aside, declaring them to be, as the lawyers would say, *void for inconsistency.* I could wish that these words might cost McClellan the loss of the votes of some Peace Democrats. But I have no idea that they will. These Peace Democrats know their man, and they are as sure of their one George as of the other. Hence, whilst nothing McClellan can say in favor of a war policy, can shake their confidence in his purpose for a Southern and pro-slavery peace, the more he shall say in favor of such policy the more will he rise in their esteem—all that he so says passing to the credit of his cunning in catching the votes of War Democrats.

I am not ignorant that the *Daily News* and *Metropolitan Record,* Vallandigham and other such, have come out against McClellan. But they will be for him when election comes. Why

3

should they not be? Why should they not trust him? Like
them he slanders the Government and the North. Like them, instead of ever saying so much as one word against slavery, he is constantly proving that his great concern is to save it. It is true
that their treason is more open and noisy than his, but his is nevertheless as real and earnest as theirs. The coming out of Peace
Democrats against McClellan is most likely but part of the game.
Their showing a want of confidence in him is expected to increase
the confidence of War Democrats in him. But even if there are
a few Peace Democrats, who, because of the warlike words in his
letter, do not like to vote for him, they nevertheless will vote for
him. Such fellows are always either coaxed or whipped in. Let not
the friends of the country flatter themselves that McClellan, who
is in heart just what the Peace Democrats could wish him to be,
will lose so much as one of their votes.

I pass on to inquire why it is, since the South is so obviously
the guilty party in this war, so large a share of the Northern people goes with her. It is because of the power of party. It was
long ago that the Democratic party came into alliance with slavery. I do not believe that it was, as a prominent politician in effect declared it to be, a "natural" alliance. In the early days of
the Republic the parties, morally considered, were not essentially
different. But its espousal of the pro-slavery policy wrought a
sad change in the Democratic party. Its good men saw it and
lamented it; and from time to time many of them quit it. When
at length slavery, having failed to accomplish its ends by political, commercial, and ecclesiastical agencies, burst forth in rebellion,
(for the rebellion is neither more nor less than slavery in arms,)
then, as was to be expected, there was a great exodus from the
Democratic party. Thousands of that party, who had been guilty of falling in with its concessions to slavery, hoping thereby not
only to help their party but to preserve the quiet and promote
the prosperity of the country, could no longer remain in their pro-
slavery party after slavery had undertaken the violent dismem-
berment of the nation. Nevertheless, the Democratic party did not
become weak. As is natural, those who clung to it, became more
than ever devoted to slavery : and the more pro-slavery the party became, the more attractive was it to the aristocratic element
in our population. For aristocracy, not in England only, but the
world over, must ever be in sympathy with slaveholding. Contempt of the toiling poor, black or white, bond or free, is common
to both. Moreover, as the Democratic party increased in devotion to slavery, it grew in favor with those ignorant and debased
multitudes, who love slavery because they love to have a stratum
of humanity still lower than their own. Again, these multitudes
go for slavery because they are taught by the demagogues, who
get their votes, that the colored people not in slavery are their
rivals for the humble forms of labor.

The Democratic party, now so openly and shamelessly the servant of the slave-power as to be at work either to break up the

nation or to bring all parts of it equally under the reign of slavery, has long been the servant of that power. Instance its innumerable mobs to prevent or break up the discussion of slavery. To embarrass the Government and help the rebels, it has become the champion of the right of free speech. Nevertheless, its Amos Kendall, who is now so conspicuously on the side of free speech, went so far the other way as to let slavery stalk into the Post-Office Department, and wield its mighty machinery against free speech. Even our bland and gentle Governor Seymour, who is now so distressfully concerned for the safety of free speech, was, but little more than three years ago, planning in conclave with kindred spirits the forcible prevention of a speech against slavery.

That the Democratic party should, even now, when all Christendom is giving up slavery, still cling to it, is not unaccountable. Its whole life has come to be in slavery: and it knows that when slavery dies it must itself die. Hence to expect the Democratic party to give up slavery, is to expect it to give up itself: and the political party has not yet been which will consent to give up itself.

The Democratic party is, in short, neither more nor less than the Northern wing of the rebellion : and the same spirit of opposition to universal freedom and to the lifting up of oppressed and degraded humanity, which imbues the Southern rebels, imbues the Northern rebels also. That such a party should do what it can to hinder the putting down of the rebellion is only what might be expected. But that even so guilty a party should taunt us with incompetence to carry on the war and with lack of success in it is a meanness and hypocrisy, which it surely did not need to add to its stupendous wickedness. How multiplied are its hinderances to our successful prosecution of the war! It discourages enlistments. It opposes drafts, and goes so far as to make them occasions for plundering and murderous riots. It impeaches the national credit, and does all it can to shake confidence and prevent investments in Government bonds. It slanders and vilifies our upright and able President and his upright and able Cabinet. Whilst sullen over the victories achieved by our army, it exaggerates and rejoices in its defeats. I need specify no further. Enough is it to add that its crimes and character are summed up in the crowning infamy of a Convention, which built that traitorous and hypocritical platform, and put upon it the two Georges, who are precisely suited to it and to each other. How sad that the men, who are doing these things, are even too depraved and too infatuated to pause and consider what a heritage of shame they are preparing for their children.

The friends of the country must not allow themselves to be discouraged by all that its Northern and therefore its worst enemies have done and are still doing to discourage them. They must continue to believe that a cause, so good as is their cause, will not fail. They must still have faith in God, and still believe that He will not suffer the hard-earned treasure and righteous blood, which we have poured out in the war to be but waste. They must still believe that our brave and dear soldiers and sailors, who have died or been crippled in this war, have not died nor been crippled in vain. They must still believe that the sorrows of our scores of thousands of bereaved families will find their soothing and recompense in a nation of all its former boundaries and of far more than all its former justice, freedom, and prosperity.

This nation will live. It has given ample proof that it can withstand both foreign and domestic foes, both Northern and Southern rebels. This nation will live to see herself and the whole continent free from oppressors—not from slaveholders only but from imperial despots also. The Democratic party will not much longer, by weakening and disgracing us, encourage the designs of the Napoleons and Maximilians. For the Democratic party will soon die. As life is the law of righteousness, so death is the law of wickedness; and the wickedness of the Democratic party is fast nearing that extreme limit where wickedness, all ripe and rotten, dies of itself.

Let us be of good cheer. Atlanta is already ours. So also is the bay of Mobile. Very soon we shall have conquered two or three other important points; and then but a brief, feeble, flickering life will remain to the rebellion. What is scarcely less important, the election will also be ours. And then, thanks to God, the Democratic party, that ugliest of all the enemies of human rights and human happiness, will be dead. The name may survive; but the party that shall wear it will be as unlike to the present Democratic party, as day is to darkness.

PETERBORO, September 14, 1864.

LETTER TO MR. KIRKLAND.

PETERBORO, September 24, 1864.

CHARLES P. KIRKLAND, Esq., New-York:

MY FRIEND AND COLLEGE-MATE: I have read your Address on the "Destiny of our Country," and I thank you for sending it to me. Parts of it I like, and parts of it I dislike.

1st. I like your clear and forcible view of the cause of the rebellion. Entirely do I agree with you that the one cause of it is slavery, and the anti-democratic, ambitious, aristocratic spirit which it produces.

2d. Your flings at the abolitionists I do not like. Your grandchildren will not like them. For in their day when the land shall be redeemed from the debauchment of slavery, and "abolitionist" shall have become the most honored and popular of all the names in it, there will be deep regret that beloved ancestors, who should themselves have been zealous abolitionists, knew no better than to despise abolitionists. It has ever been so, that the prophets are not recognized by their generation. Those were not, who warned the Jews of the coming ruin. Nor were those, who foretold the sufferings and sorrows, that would surely befall this nation, should she persist in oppression. Alas! not even now, when their abundant prophecies are being so abundantly and so horridly fulfilled, have you, my old friend, a heart to do them honor, or even to spare them from derision and reprobation! You denounce their fanaticism and couple it with the Satanic fanaticism of the rebels. You make fun of their fewness; and tell that their candidate for Governor of this State got but five thousand votes. He and his associates labored for many years to induce the people of the North to withhold their votes from slaveholders and pro-slavery men. Oh! had they but succeeded! There would have been no rebellion then! It was the pro-slavery voters of the North that encouraged the South in her pro-slavery schemes: and but for her reliance on those voters, she would not have ventured on rebellion. Let but our infamously pro-slavery and traitorous Democratic party desert her, and she would quickly desert her then hopeless cause. Nay, but for her hope (vain hope!) of McClellan's election, she would regard her present straits as desperate, and think it time to give up the contest.

By the way, your great contempt of the abolitionists has kept you quite ignorant of their history. For instance, you suppose that those five thousand were all opponents of the Constitution. Probably not one of them was. Their candidate had never written nor spoken a word against the Constitution : and few persons had written or spoken so much for it. Improbable, is it, therefore, that any of them would have voted for him had they not, like him, been for the Constitution—for the Constitution just as it is. I admit that there are abolitionists who dislike the Constitution. William Lloyd Garrison and Wendell Phillips are such : and where shall we look for men more intellectual or pure than Mr. Garrison and Mr. Phillips ?

3d. I like your saying that our first work " is to crush the rebellion." But what men have engaged in this work more earnestly than the abolitionists ? Nay, is it not true that the negroes and the abolitionists North and South, are the only classes whose zeal against the rebellion is never called in question ? No time then is this for a patriot (and you are a patriot) to be holding up the abolitionists to hatred and ridicule. On the contrary, we should stand by all those who, in this hour of her peril stand by the country.

4th. I dislike your looking beyond this work of crushing the rebellion. All the true friends of the country are fellow-laborers in this work. But beyond it are things about which they will disagree—or at least about which they would now disagree. These things should therefore be left until we come to them. To bring them up now, is to impair our indispensable unity. Moreover, we are too fully occupied with the cares of the present to be justified in adding to them what is in the future, and what we shall best understand when, in the order of events, we shall have reached it. As you now feel, the preserving of the entire letter of the Constitution would be your first care after the rebellion had been put down. But another man might think that his first care after it, would be the setting up of new securities against further rebellious outbreaks. The salvation of a country rather than the salvation of a paper would be his paramount concern. Again, you would, as you now think, hold that the conquered rebels must still be in the Union. But another person would hold that it would be for their conqueror to decide the point—to recognize them as in the Union if he pleased, or out of it if that were his preference. Again, you probably believe that, on their professed re-submission to the Constitution, the rebel States would, of necessity, return to the enjoyment of all constitutional rights. But another believes that, when they rebelled, they forfeited entirely and forever every constitutional right: and that, if we conquer them, they will be as absolutely at our disposal as if they had never been under the Constitution—nay, as absolutely as if they had been a part of Canada or Mexico, instead of our own country. To bring forward one more illustration. You would allow such acts of the President in this war as were performed in the capacity of Head of the Army and Navy to be submitted to the Supreme Court of the United States. But another would differ from you—and this, too, notwithstanding both the President and Secretary of State are with you at that point. He might admit that a local insurrection, affecting a county, or even so serious as to spread its disturbing influence over a State, could and therefore should be met by constitutional law only—by that law of which that Court is the acknowledged interpreter. But he would not admit the sufficiency of that law, nor therefore the jurisdiction of that Court, in all that arises in such a war as this, which is upon our hands—a war in which our foe is a people of territory and resources enough to make them a mighty nation—a war which was scarcely begun ere several nations accorded belligerent rights to that foe, and which, very soon after, we ourselves could not withhold. The conduct of such a war he would bring under the broad principles of international law. Or rather, he would say that no written law can provide for the exigencies of such a war—and that the war must be a law unto itself. Moreover, he might put some perplexing questions to you. He might ask you—why, if the President's military acts can be reviewed by the Supreme Court, General Grant's and General Sherman's can not also. He might ask you whether you hold it to be competent for that Court to entertain the complaints of this and that man for being compelled to give up their houses and barns to soldiers and soldiers' horses. Observe that I do not say which of you is right. Perhaps, both of you, when our nation shall, in her present perilous journey, have reached these questions, will find your present views of them somewhat modified. Do not, dear Kirkland, be impatient to commit the people to your views of these questions. Leave it to that traitorous band, who at Chicago made their traitorous platform, and put upon it their traitorous candidates, to embarrass the Administration, and distract the people and hinder their undivided and effective prosecution of the war by the premature discussion of these questions.

Trusting that your heart is set on the election of the honest and able patriot, Mr. Lincoln; and that neither McClellan, nor any other candidate who belongs to the Northern wing of the rebellion, finds any favor in your sight,

I remain your friend,
GERRIT SMITH.

TO THE RANK AND FILE OF THE DEMOCRATIC PARTY.

PETERBORO, October 20, 1864.

To THE MASSES OF THE DEMOCRATIC PARTY:

I HAVE faith that you will hear me—first, because I am an old man, and past being suspected of seeking personal political advantage; second, because, being no partisan, and having never belonged to the Democratic, Whig, nor Republican party, I am not liable to the charge of seeking party objects.

You, like all multitudes of men, love justice and love your country. Nevertheless, this does not assure me that, in the approaching election, you will be faithful to either. For, trained as you are to implicit confidence in the leaders of your party, there is but too much reason to fear that you will follow them even now, when to follow them is to be their instruments in outraging righteousness and ruining your country.

In the breasts of politicians where ambition, the greed of gain and the lust of place and power have usually so much play, justice and patriotism are apt to become weak. But in the breasts of *your* political leaders these virtues seem to have become absolutely extinct. Step by step they have gone on courting and conceding to the slave power, until at last they are so debauched as to be no longer capable of withholding any thing from its claims. When the South at the instigation of that power broke out in this rebellion against a nation, which had done her no harm, save the harm of weakly and wickedly indulging her and succumbing to her, these leaders were as yet able to make, or at least to seem to make, some resistance. But now they have got so far along in the way of evil, as distinctly to take the side of the rebellion; as openly and shamelessly to join the rebels, and employ every art to induce you also to join them.

For proof that your leaders have gone over to the enemy, I refer not to the obvious fact that they are at work with him to defame, embarrass, and destroy our Government; to the obvious fact that the spirit of the Democratic press in Philadelphia, New-York, Boston, and elsewhere, is one with the spirit of the Southern press; to the obvious fact that your leaders rejoice with the South in her successes, and sorrow with her in her defeats; to the obvious fact that, whilst the South shoots and starves our soldiers, your leaders, in denouncing the drafts and in various other ways, hinder the replenishing of our wasted armies; and, by impeaching the credit and cheapening the bonds of the Government, enfeeble its prosecution of the war ; nor to the obvious fact that they are equally intent with the South on upholding slavery, which is the one cause of the rebellion. Nor have I reference to the obvious fact that the South identifies the cause of the Democratic party with her own cause, and that whilst she looks to our coming election as fraught with triumph or ruin to her rebellion, she also regards her own fortune as decisive of the fate of that party. Says the Charleston *Courier:* " Our success in battle insures the success of McClellan. Our failure will inevitably lead to his defeat."

But there is evidence far more conclusive than any or all of this which I have cited that the leaders of your party have identified themselves with the rebellion. God grant that they may not succeed in identifying you also with it ! Go with me to the Chicago Convention. Look at the platform which it built, or rather which it adopted—for it was probably mainly built on the British side of the Niagara, if not indeed in Richmond. It says nothing against the South. It abounds in complaints of the North. It is at peace with the South, and at war with the North. It pronounces the war on our part a failure—and this, too, when the South is reduced to far less than half the territory she began the rebellion with, and our final success seems so near at hand. It calls for the stopping of the war. But a poorer time is it to *stop* than " to swap horses, when crossing the stream." More is the danger that they will be swept down-stream. To stop the war now, is to forego the object of the war—the deliverance of the nation from threatened death. To stop it now, is to lose all the blood and treasure it has cost. To stop it now, is to make vain and to leave unrecompensed the bereavements and desolations, which tens of thousands of our families have suffered from it. And for what end could the war be stopped now, but to abandon it and to leave the rebellion to triumph ? Is it said, that opportunity will thus be afforded for the calm and wise consideration of the questions between the North and South ? But there are no questions between them, and there can be none until the South has laid down her arms. Until then, she has no right to be heard, and we have no right to hear her. Until then, neither party has the right to propose conditions of peace. The South took up arms without cause. She must lay them down without conditions. Until then, any negotiations with her—even such *quasi* negotiations, as our excellent President has in the weakness of his goodness countenanced—would be at the expense of dishonoring justice and compromising the dignity and sacredness of nationality. General McClellan thinks " we should exhaust all the resources of statesmanship to secure peace." But until peace there is nothing for statesmanship to act on. Until then, it must be *generalship* instead of statesmanship, *fighting* instead of negotiation. Afterward many ques-

tions will arise in the province of statesmanship: and I trust that
our Government will be disposed to treat them all justly and,
where need be, generously also.

It will held by some that there is one question between the
North and the South, even while they are at war with each other.
It is that of exchanging prisoners. But I do not see that even
here there is room for a question. By the laws of war neither
party to the war can be required to consent to an exchange of
prisoners. Each may retain all its prisoners to the end of the
war. If the South does, for any reasons, value her black prisoners too highly to consent to exchange them for her white men in
our hands, so be it, and we have no right to complain. If she con-
sents to however limited an exchange of prisoners, black or white,
we are to thank her, and for humanity's sake to rejoice. The
wrong treatment of prisoners is another subject, and one with
which this should not be complicated, nor on which it should in
the slightest degree be made to depend. If the South shall abuse
any of her prisoners—if, for instance, she shall starve or kill, or
what is worse, sink them in slavery, it is for us and us only to decide what shall be the return or retaliation for the outrage. All
this, however, has nothing to do with the exchange of prisoners.

But to return from this digression. We were speaking of the
Chicago Platform. One of the things, which the Convention did
after adopting it, was to put George H. Pendleton upon it. Pre-
eminently fitted to it is he. Vallandigham himself could not be
more so. From the first, Pendleton has been openly on the side
of the rebels. On the floor of Congress in January, 1861, when
several States had already seceded, he denied our right to compel
the return of a seceding State. In harmony with this denial his
subsequent votes have been against condemning the rebellion and
against providing means for carrying on the war to suppress it.
This is the rebel, whom your leaders would have you try to make
Vice-President. Can you try it without becoming rebels yourselves? He is the exponent of the Chicago Platform. In the
light of his speeches and votes, whatever is obscure or doubtful
in that platform becomes clear and certain. Can you consent to
commit the Democratic party to a platform so entirely in the interest of the rebellion?

You perhaps wonder that I have omitted to mention the nomination of McClellan. But I was describing and illustrating the
Chicago Platform: and his nomination has nothing to do with
that peace platform. His name was chosen, not to represent
the platform, but as the bait for catching the votes of War Democrats. It was a trick—as mere a trick as the Baltimore Convention would have been guilty of, had it baited for peace votes by
putting a non-resistant Quaker on its thorough war platform. I
grant that the nomination of McClellan was a very cunning trick.
For whilst, on the one hand, his having had a part in the war
would commend him to the votes of War Democrats, that part,
on the other hand, was so equivocal, so tender, and advantageous

to the enemy, as not to deter Peace Democrats from voting for him.

And now, what are the arguments, which the leaders of the Democratic party, its orators and presses, employ to bring you to abandon the cause of your country and to identify yourselves with the rebels? Only two which they greatly rely on, or which it is worth while for me to notice. The first is the perversion of the war from the putting down of the rebellion to the putting down of slavery. The second is the cost of carrying on the war—the cost in money and the cost in life.

First. I do not deny that one-idea abolitionists desired the perversion. But I do deny that their desire was gratified. From first to last, the Government has withstood all the clamor and all the influence for the perversion.

The leading doctrine of that admirable letter of August twenty-second, 1862, from President Lincoln to Horace Greeley, in which he shows his clear understanding of the limitations upon his military power is, that he would emancipate slaves no farther than he sees it to be a necessity for saving his country. Surely, this doctrine does not justify the charge of perverting the war.

The President's Proclamation of September twenty-second, 1862, sets out the declaration "that hereafter as heretofore the war will be prosecuted for the object of practically restoring the constitutional relation," etc. No perversion of the war in this declaration. But this Proclamation contains a threat of Emancipation! Yes, but the threat is to be fulfilled only in case the rebels refuse to lay down their arms. Does such a threat pervert the war? So far from it, it is in the very line of the original and legitimate war. His Proclamation of January first, 1863, does, so far as it can, fulfill this threat. Did the fulfillment pervert the war? Oh! no. It weakened the foe and strengthened ourselves. It gave us new means for carrying on the war against him, and, like all our previous means for carrying it on, they have been faithfully used to that one end.

But your leaders tell you that the war has been perverted by bringing black men into the army. I doubt not that many of these black men are inspired with the hope that the putting down of the rebellion will be the putting down of slavery. All the fiercer, therefore, will they fight to put down the rebellion. Hence no perversion of the war need be feared at their hands: and so far from encouraging the cry of perversion, we should be thankful that scores of thousands of these brave and stalwart black men are found willing to help us release our country from the bloody grasp of rebels. Thankful should we be to these defenders of our homes that they save us from the necessity of defending them ourselves. A hundred thousand black soldiers save fifty thousand Unionists and fifty thousand Democrats from being soldiers. I do not deny that it is a great trial to the Southern chivalry, with whom your leaders so tenderly sympathize, to have to fight with negroes. I do not deny that it must be very humiliating and ex-

asperating to Southern gentlemen to find themselves confronted
on the battle-field by their former slaves. But before taking up
arms to destroy the best form of government the world ever saw
and to dismember a nation that had never done them the least
harm, they should have foreseen that, sooner than consent to perish under their parricidal blows, we would summon to our aid red
and black as well as white men.   Much and basely as we had, in
the past, studied to please the slaveholders, they should have
foreseen that when the alternative before us was to save their
pride or save our country, we could not long hesitate which to
choose.

Second. The other argument of your leaders why you should
abandon the war and join the rebels is, as I have said, the cost of
carrying on the war. I admit the cost is great. Still is it not
better for us to go through with the war, and to reach final victory as we can do in a few months, and as a united North, un-
cursed with disloyal demagogues and disloyal generals, could
have done more than two years ago? In that case we should
have but our own debt to pay; and no small share of that we
should be enabled to pay from confiscation of the estates of the
wealthy men involved in the rebellion. The possessions of the
poor we would be too pitiful and generous to molest. But in the
event of the success of the Democratic party at the coming election and of the consequent immediate stopping of the war, or in
other words of the abandonment of the war, or in still other
words, of the success of the rebellion, the doctrines of State sovereignty and State secession would be triumphant. Then the
whole Democratic party would declare with George II. Pendleton
that our Government has no right to coërce seceded States; and
then it would also declare that we are equitably bound to pay
those States all the expense we have put them to in resisting our
unconstitutional coërcion. Thus, by giving up the war we should,
instead of staying the increase of our debt, double it; and instead
of our getting remuneration from the South, she would get remuneration from the North.

As to life—we would, it is true, stay the loss of it by stopping
the war. But the war stopped now, or at any time before the
rebellion is subdued, would speedily break out afresh, and lead to
a sacrifice of life many fold greater than would be necessary to
prosecute it to a decisive result from our present vantage-ground.

I am not, however, willing to argue this point on this low
ground only. I hold that we must, at whatever cost, carry on the
war to final victory or final defeat. It is a case where we have
no option, and no right to stop to count the cost. We must persevere until we have subdued the rebellion, or been subdued by
it. If need be, we must persevere until men and money and credit
shall all fail us. Infinitely honorable would it be for our nation to exhaust herself and perish in her struggle to crush this
most infernal of all rebellions. But infamous to the last degree,
and forever would she be, were she to consent to prolong her life

by a compromise with the guiltiest of rebels and by recognizing their nationality alongside of her own. Our nation can afford to die an honorable death—but she can not afford to live a dishonorable life.

Your leaders say we can not pay our present debt. The mineral wealth of the country is sufficient to pay it in thirty years. Our gold and silver mines will yield the present year more than a hundred millions of dollars. By the time we shall have reached the fourth or fifth year of peace, they will yield double this sum. Scarcely less will be the yield of our iron, copper, lead, tin, quicksilver, salt, and coal.

Your leaders seek to alarm you by telling you that rich England groans under a debt scarcely twice as large as our own. How idle to compare England's productiveness with our own!—little England with this nation, which stretches from sea to sea—little England that half a century hence will not have one third of the population we shall then have. Of course, I am not taking into the account her colonies. These gratify her pride and ambition; but they do little toward helping her pay debts. Is her trade with them lucrative? So would it be, were they not her colonies.

And, to make our prospect the more gloomy and despairing, your leaders dwell on our town and county bounty-money burdens. But so far from regarding as burdens the bounties we give those who arm themselves for our defense, we should rejoice in their wealth-distributing and wealth-equalizing office. They take from those who have, to give to those who have not, and to those too, whose patriotic and perilous services can not be overpaid. What right-minded person does not rejoice when seeing those bounty-moneys procure homes for families who never before had homes? — and when seeing these families lifted up for the first time to a comfortable grade of living? Your leaders speak of the aggregate of those bounty-moneys as so much that the nation has parted with and lost. But it is still in the nation to help pay her debts with—and what is more, it is in hands where it does far greater good than it did before. In this connection let me add that a very considerable share of the great debt, which the Government owes, is for profits, which have been realized in the contracts made with it and in the purchase of its bonds. These profits, like the bounty-moneys, are still in the nation, and, like them, will help the nation pay its debt. Moreover, it is these profits, which have, during the war, so stimulated the industry of the nation, and given such unprecedented prosperity to all its branches.

But what, you will inquire, can be the motive of the Democratic leaders in bringing their party to the side of the rebellion? I answer, that it is the same with that which prompted the rebellion—in other words, that the motive is *to save slavery*. The authors of the rebellion—of the greatest crime of all the nations and all the ages—saw that the progressive civilization of Christendom boded destruction to slavery. They saw that it was cast out of Europe; that it was nearly extinct in her colonies; that it was tottering in Brazil; and becoming more hateful in our Northern States. Hence they resolved to insulate themselves and their slavery. In order to keep fast, forever fast, the chains upon a race as innocent as hapless, they undertook to build up around both slaves and masters the walls of a new nationality — walls so high that the outside and growing anti-slavery sentiment could not leap over—walls so impervious that it could not pass through. Herein and herein alone is the explanation of the rebellion.

Now, as the slaveholders have their life — the life of their ease and luxury, and ambition, and tyranny — the life of all their habits—in slavery, so also the Democratic party had, from its long-continued alliance with slaveholders and long-continued dependence upon them, come to have its life in slavery. Hence the leaders of that party, though, at the first, quite generally opposed to the rebellion, came to sympathize with it as soon as they saw that its downfall involved the downfall of slavery. For, they well knew that when slavery should die, the Democratic party would also die. Blessed be God that slavery is to die! Blessed be God that it is to die, if it be only that the most demoralizing and devilish of all the political parties, which ever cursed mankind, is to die with it! The approaching election will cast into a common grave, and that grave too deep to allow of a resurrection, Slavery, Rebellion, and the Democratic party. Doubtless there will still be a Democratic party. But it will not be the devil which this one is—for it will be dissevered from slavery.

I frequently see in the Democratic newspapers extracts from the speeches and writings of such men as Daniel S. Dickinson, Benjamin F. Butler, and Lyman Tremain. These extracts are to prove that they were once as pro-slavery as are the remaining leaders of the Democratic party. But this is as unreasonable and shameless as for remaining drunkards to reproach reformed drunkards with their former history and habits. For one, I honor and love such men as Dickinson and Butler and Tremain, and should be glad to see them advanced to higher and higher places of trust and power. For, notwithstanding they were, in common with the other leaders of their party, victims of the most abominable political education, they had conscience enough left to stand aghast at the culminating wickedness of their party, and to quit their party;—or, if you prefer, involving them in personal as well as party guilt, conscience enough left to stand aghast at their own wickedness, and to repent of it and forsake it. Alas! this pride of consistency; this pride in never changing! How vulgar and vicious and vile it is! When will it be seen, that the duty of all of us—of even the best of us—is to be ever and ever changing, be it only toward the right! When will it be seen, that man is among his best and sublimest employments, when writing with his own finger condemnation upon his own erring and guilty past! Dickinson and Butler and Tremain had the courage to change. They stepped upward, and saved themselves, and became saviours of their country. To remain where they were, would have been to remain destroyers of themselves and their country.

I stated the arguments with which your leaders ply you, and by force of which they hope to bring you to the side of the rebels. The first one appeals to those prejudices against the black man, which they have so industriously and, alas! so successfully cultivated in you. They hope that, under the sway of those strong prejudices, you would rather that the rebellion should triumph, than that the slave should go free. But have you not hated him long enough? He is denied all right to learning and honors and child and wife and himself and his earnings. And yet his despised black skin covers a heart as warm to all these relations and interests as does your own proud white one. Tell your leaders, I beseech you — your tempters and seducers — that their appeal to your hatred of the negro will be vain. Tell them that he has suffered long enough; that you have hated and wronged him long enough; and that you are more disposed to repent of your part in crushing him than to persist in it. Tell them, in a word, that you have come to believe more in your obligation to honor God and all the varieties of the human family than in your obligation to serve ambitious and greedy demagogues.

The other argument which, I said, your leaders employ to bring you to join the rebels, is the cost of carrying on the war. Their hope of success at this point is in your selfishness and lack of patriotism. They flatter themselves that you had rather lose the country than have your property taxed to save it: and that, rather than let your sons go, or go yourselves into the hardships and perils of war, you would let the rebellion and slavery sweep over and blast the whole land. Disappoint them here also, I entreat you. Tell them that of all the claims, which earth can make upon your property, that, which your imperiled country makes upon it, is paramount. Tell them that to be poor and yet have a country, is to be rich—whilst to be rich and yet to be stripped of country, is to be poor. Tell them, too, that you have laid your sons and yourselves upon the altar of your country, and that you count death in her service not as dreadful, but as blessed.

How elevating and ennobling is this war to all who have a heart to go forth to its unselfish, patriotic, and sublime duties! But how sinking and shriveling is it to all those who shrink from these duties, and prefer to cower in their cowardice, and to shut themselves in the shell of their selfishness!

EXTRACT FROM A DISCOURSE IN PETERBORO,

NOVEMBER 20, 1864.

———•♦•———

"I NEED say no more to show how necessary to true religion
and to the best type of manhood is unwavering fidelity to the
claims of nature. Were I called on for the most striking and
melancholy instance of trampling on these claims, I would cite
the late Democratic party. I say *late*, for it is dead : and slavery and the rebellion, instead of being able to raise their ally
to life again, will soon be in the same grave with it. I do not
say that there will never again be a Democratic party amongst us.
There will be. It will not, however, be like the old one. For
slavery, the soul of the old one, will not be alive to animate the
new one. Nor will it be the party which was proposed in the
War Democratic Meeting held in New-York a few days before
the recent election. For that would be a party, if not too cowardly, nevertheless, too prudent, to speak of slavery. Most emphatically would that party furnish an instance of the playing of
Hamlet with the part of Hamlet left out. The saying that never
more can a man who spells 'negro' with two 'g's' become
President, is a very true one. As true, however, is it that no
party, which, whilst slavery lasts, favors or ignores it, will ever
again be in the ascendant. No, the Democratic party which
shall succeed the deceased one, will be impartial toward all the
varieties of the human family, and be based on equal justice toward all men. The original Democratic party, that of Jefferson's
day, and, in no small degree, of his making, was worthy of honor.
The late Democratic party had no title whatever to its prestige
or traditions. It was a thief. But, unlike most thieves, (for
they take what is most valuable and leave what is least so,) it
took the name and left the principles of the original Democratic
party ; the flag, and left all it symbolized. That with this name
and flag it was able to juggle so successfully and to accomplish
so much evil, is, to say the least, very discreditable to the
popular intelligence. I have praised the original Democratic
party : but the Democratic party which is to come will be a far
better one.

" We return from this digression, and proceed in showing how frightfully at war with nature was the late Democratic party; in other words, how frightfully unnatural it was. Slavery not only robs its victim of every right, but with unapproachable blasphemy it attempts a change—an entire change—in his essential, God-given being. It drags him down from the glorious heights of humanity to class him with brutes and things. It reduces immortality to merchandise. Such is the hideous, the stupendous crime against nature of which the slaveholder is guilty. There is only one other on earth that is more hideous, more stupendous. This one other is, when a great political party indorses and espouses slavery, and makes its perpetuation and indefinite extension its chief and vital policy. Of this greater crime against nature the late Democratic party was guilty. More than thirty years ago it began its alliance with slavery; and ere long that alliance had ripened into indissolubleness. When the rebellion broke out—when, in other words, slavery took up arms—the party, bad as it was, was somewhat shocked. Many, including of course its best men, quit it. The party did not—certainly not to a great extent—immediately and openly favor the rebellion. But, soon after, it came to see that the downfall of the rebellion would of necessity involve the downfall of slavery, and therefore its own downfall, its own life being bound up in the life of slavery. And then it delayed not to take open steps toward the side of the rebellion. At Chicago it formally and shamelessly identified itself with it. It adopted a rebellion platform—a platform at peace with the South and at war with the North. It left no material difference between itself and the Southern rebels, save the geographical one. Those were the Southern and it was the Northern wing of the rebellion.

" As proof how clearly the late Democratic party saw itself to be living in the life of slavery, and as proof, too, that its members are trained to make its interest their supreme interest, there was probably, when that party entered upon the recent election, not one man in it who was in favor of abolishing slavery, that greatest crime against God and man.

" Not a few of the Southern presses of the Democratic party held that slavery is the appropriate condition of all manual laborers. But so deep and revolting a crime against nature is slavery, that it was not easy to spread the conviction at the North that slavery is right. Nevertheless, the negroes must be continued in slavery. This was vital in the policy of the Democratic party. Hence with ceaseless industry did that party inculcate hatred of the race on whom slavery had fastened. For it knew that the more men hated this innocent and hapless race the more they would be reconciled to its enslavement, and the less they would speak of and pity its wrongs. The first and last and never-ceasing lesson which that party taught Irish immigrants was hatred, murderous hatred, of the negro. Nothing went so far to inflame it as that party's incessant lie that the negro, released from slav-

4

cry, would come North and take away the Irishman's labor. This hatred became the ruling passion of those immigrants. Under its sway they denied the right of the negro to eat or sit, or even fight for 'his country, by the side of a white man. Moreover, under its sway seven eighths of them voted with the Democratic party. The reason commonly assigned why these immigrants increase so slowly in knowledge and rise so slowly in character, is that they are Irish. I deny that this is the true reason. My respect for the memory of a grandparent born in Cork denies it. The obvious truth in the case denies it. Why these immigrants are so backward in knowledge and character is chiefly because they were made into Democrats and drank in the Democratic hatred of the negro. Need any one be told that hatred is shriveling to the soul which harbors it? Need any one be told that, had these immigrants been taught love, instead of hatred, they would have expanded into a wisdom and morality widely contrasting with their present intellectual and moral darkness?

" It is not because these immigrants are Irish that, so soon after landing upon our shores, they show themselves to be the deadly oppressors of our harmless and helpless colored people. It is because they are scarcely landed ere they are, as I said before, made into Democrats. Would that it were into real Democrats! But, alas, it is into the Satanic style of Democrats! The people of Ireland are taught to hate oppression by their own suffering of it. They hate it when they come to us. But very soon, under Democratic appliances, they are made ready to practice it.

" Chief-Justice Taney was much censured for favoring the sentiment that black men have no rights which white men are bound to respect. But he was pushed up to it by the Democratic party. This sentiment had long been the sentiment of that party. A practice corresponding with it had long been the practice of that party. Within a few weeks the Chief-Justice has left our world. There is a world (and may be he has gone to it) where to condemn a man for his skin is held to be a mistake; and where those few words of dear Robert Burns, "A man's a man for a' that," infinitely outweigh all the nonsense and blasphemy which pro-slavery courts and pro-slavery parties and pro-slavery churches have uttered to the contrary.

" It is held that the Catholic priests help the Democratic party to the Irish vote. I am not prepared to believe it. Like the ministers of the Episcopal Church, they stand aloof from politics. I would myself that all preachers preached politics—the politics of wisdom, justice, and humanity. For to me, it is as plain that pure politics are a part of religion as that the theologies are not. Deeply do I rejoice that most of the ministers of most of the sects have of late years come to preach politics. God bless them for their good service in this wise in the last election! Great and blessed is this change! Only twenty years ago, and they were strenuously opposed to bringing politics into the pulpit; and if a layman ventured to attempt to supply their delinquency, he lost all favor with them. Our ministers are making religion more practical; and the more they do so, the more will their interest in the theologies decline. Compared with his interest in practical righteousness—in other phrase, with his interest in religion—how little does Henry Ward Beecher care for the theologies! What a contrast between the dry, dogmatic, useless sermons of the last century and the juicy and fit-for-use sermons of the present day!

"That a party, which has its life in slavery, should furnish tens of thousands of men to those secret, oath-bound, bloody Associations that are coöperating with Southern rebels; and that, under its educating influences, there should come forth men base and villainous enough to attempt the ruin of their country by forgeries upon soldiers and frauds upon the ballot-box, is but what might have been expected. So, too, it was but a matter of course that such a party should be exceedingly attractive to the vicious and ignorant. Of the drunkards and of the men who can not read and write, who voted at the late election, probably seven eighths voted Democratic tickets. Those localities in our great cities which are sinks of vice have generally given their almost entire vote to the Democratic party. Cunning and corruption combined with ignorance, and ceaselessly playing upon it—these were so largely the elements in the Democratic party, that one might almost say they made up the party. And these were the elements that made it both numerous and strong. But happily the strength, which comes of such sources, is short-lived, whilst that which is founded in virtue and intelligence, is permanent.

"Am I asked whether there were no good men in the Democratic party? I answer that there were tens of thousands. Many of them were blind to its bad character. Many of them continued in it simply from the force of habit. They had always been in the Democratic party; and though the change which had taken place in it was as great as from day to night, they must nevertheless continue in it. That the ship was rotten and sinking, did not arrest their attention. That it carried the same name and flag, as that which had gone triumphantly through so many tempests, was enough to assure them of safety and keep them from deserting it.

"And how do I explain the fact that thousands of intelligent, high-minded, cultivated gentlemen, who, though well knowing what the Democratic party was, nevertheless consented to belong to it? I answer that it was *because* they knew what it was, that they belonged to it. They had so far smothered their nature with their conventionalisms as to become unnatural enough to feel at home in so unnatural a party. They had drawn a broad line of demarkation between themselves and the masses—especially between themselves and the poor, most of all, the negroes, who are the poorest of the poor. In a word, they were aristocrats, and therefore could not fail of a strong affinity for the most aristocratic party in the world. They had that contempt of the

poor which is the leading element in aristocracy; and so strong
was it in that party, as to make increasingly popular in it the
doctrine that the rich should own the poor and capital own labor.
Not strange was it, then, that the aristocrats of America should
attach themselves to that party, nor strange was it that the aristocrats of Europe should sympathize with it. Nor was it strange
that both should wish success to the rebellion, since they saw it
so clear that the rebellion and negro slavery and the Democratic
party must all succeed together or fail together ; and since, too,
they saw it so clear that aristocracy would gain much by the success or lose much by the failure.

"I need say no more to justify my citing the deceased Democratic party as a preëminent instance of outrages on the principles and rights of human nature, and therefore as a striking speci-
men of the exceedingly and monstrously unnatural. Let this
party, whose malignant and untiring industry on the side of the
rebellion threatened ruin to our country; let this party, so furi-
ously at war with the claims of nature, and therefore with the
claims of religion ; let its career and its close effectually admon-
ish us to be true to humanity, and to stand by its rights in the
persons of men of whatever clime, complexion, or condition. So
shall we stand by God also ; and so will He in turn stand by us.
Nature or religion (which in this connection is a word of the
same import) succeeded at the late election. The suppression of
the rebellion and the freedom of all the slaves, highly probable
before, are made certain by this success. But whether our nation
shall be saved will turn upon the question, whether we shall be so
true to the claims of nature—to the claims of religion—as to
enthrone justice in our governments, our churches, our hearts—a
justice so impartial as to accord equal rights to all, born wherever
they may have been or with whatever complexion. A nation can
be saved only by righteousness. It is only in a low sense that as
yet any of the nations have been saved. When all of them shall
recognize and protect all the natural rights of all men, then all
of them will be saved. Then there will no longer be war, not
slavery, nor land-monopoly, nor licensed dram-shop, nor denial
to woman of civil and political equality with man. Then, indeed,
will have come the "Millennium ;" not because it was foretold,
but because it was earned. It will come not as the beginning,
but as the fruit of righteousness ; not to last for only a thousand
years, but so long as justice shall reign amongst men, and so long
as the religion of nature and reason and Jesus—the religion of
doing as we would be done by—shall be their religion."

LETTER TO SENATOR SUMNER.

— ♦ ♦ —

[Justice to the Constitution, and to the Honest Masses who Voted for it!

— ♦ ♦ —

PETERBORO, December 5, 1864.

HON. CHARLES SUMNER:

My DEAR SIR: I do not forget that to be singular is to be regarded as both eccentric and egotistical; and that to be regarded as either, is much in the way of one's usefulness. Nevertheless, I must confess that at one point in our national affairs I have never been able to fall in with the friends of freedom. I refer to their eagerness during the present year to have the Constitution amended. Allow me to call your attention to some of the reasons why I have no sympathy with this eagerness. If there is no force in them, the mention of them can do no harm. If there is, it may do good.

First. The excitement and distraction attendant on war render it an unfavorable time for the responsible and solemn work of altering the organic law of the land. For no work can the calmness, composure, and leisure which peace brings, be more necessary.

Second. During all this entirely unprovoked, this wantonly and surpassingly wicked rebellion, the duty ever nearest to us, nay, our one duty, has been to suppress it. We must not be diverted from it. We must be absorbed in it.

Of course, I admit the rightfulness, nay, the absolute obligation, of doing whatever the most faithful discharge of this duty calls for. If it calls for the total abolition of slavery, and if the power with which he is invested as head of the army does not authorize the President to respond, nevertheless Congress is abundantly authorized to make the response. The constitutional right of Congress to declare war is, of course, attended by the constitutional right to carry on war, and to carry it on by means of its own selection and by enacting laws, which itself shall judge to be "necessary and proper." To deny to Congress unlimited discretion in carrying on war, unlimited discretion over both men and property — and this too, if need be, to the extent of abolishing both slavery and apprenticeship, or even of shutting up both schools and churches—is virtually to admit that we are not a nation. Absolute power in conducting war is vital to nationality.

If our spirit of democracy, or, in other words, our jealousy and impatience of power, can not abide this absoluteness, then we had better exchange it for a spirit that can ; or frankly advertise the nations, that we shall hold ourselves an easy prey to whichever of them shall choose to make war upon us.

I do not say that, on the return of peace, slavery and apprenticeship could not be reëstablished, and the schools and churches reöpened. I speak of the power of Congress during war.

The only justification for changing the Constitution in a time so unpropitious as that of war, is that it is needful to success in the war. But it never can be needful so long as the power of Congress in carrying on war remains absolute. If, for instance, it is slavery that stands in the way of such success, then there can be congressional statutes, which will operate more speedily, and, for the present, more effectively to remove it than can any attempted constitutional changes. Is it said that the South would be more disheartened by a constitutional or permanent abolition of slavery than by a congressional or temporary abolition of it? I answer that the South is in such straits as leave her no concern but to get out of them ; that her present success is her present and so absorbing concern, as to make her indifferent to what lies beyond the rebellion.

Third. A seriously disturbing question might hereafter arise as to the constitutionality of the amendment, provided it was not assented to by three fourths of all the States, loyal and disloyal, and this too, without counting in the three fourths West-Virginia or any of the reconstructed seceded States.

Fourth. But the chief reason why I am clear of this impatience for the proposed constitutional Amendment is my strong apprehension that it will not be couched in suitable words.

An Amendment, implying that without it the Constitution would authorize or even tolerate slavery, would do great injustice to those who adopted the Constitution. It would be wickedly blotting their memory. So much stress has been laid on the history of the Constitution, it may well be said that there are two constitutions, the one the historical and the other the literal. The former is that which has ruled the country. Terrible, all the way, has been its rule. The cry of many millions to an avenging God has come of it. The soaking of our land with blood has also come of it. That the history of the Constitution has so cursed us is because it is so almost universally held to be a pro-slavery history. In other words, that this historical Constitution has so cursed us is because of the ever-urged and almost universally accepted claim that the literal Constitution was made in the interest of slavery. Alas for the people, to whom the angel of the Apocalypse cried, " wo, wo, wo !" if they suffered more than America has suffered from this historical Constitution ! That there is much for slavery in the history of the Constitution, I admit. But that there is also much in it against slavery, I affirm.

Pro-slavery interests, however, have succeeded in keeping the latter out of sight. The rejection in the Convention, which framed the Constitution, of the motion to require "fugitive slaves" to be delivered up, and the unanimous adoption, the next day, of the motion to deliver up, not "fugitive slaves," but persons from whom labor or service is *due*, is a historical fact against slavery. So, too, is Mr. Madison's unopposed declaration in the Convention that it would be "wrong to admit in the Constitution the idea that there could be property in man." And so also is that Convention's unanimous substitution of the word "service," for "servitude" for the avowed reason, that servitude expresses the condition of slaves and service that of freemen. Nothing, however, of all this did I need to say. What this thing is, which is called the history of the Constitution—what is this historical Constitution, as I have termed that history—is really of no moment. What it is in the light of the records of the Convention referred to, or of the records of the "Virginia Convention" or any other Convention ; or what it is on the pages of the *Federalist*, or of any other book, or of any newspaper, should not be made the least account of. The aggregate of all those, whose words contributed to make up this historical Constitution, is but a comparative handful. The one question is — what is the literal Constitution? For it is that, and that only, which the people adopted, and which is therefore the Constitution. They did not adopt the discussions of the Convention which framed it. These were secret. They did not adopt what the newspapers said of the Constitution. Newspapers in that day were emphatically " few and far between." But even had they been familiar with the newspapers and with the discussions, their one duty would nevertheless have been-to pass upon the simple letter of the Constitution. As Judge Story so well says : " Nothing but the text itself was adopted by the people." And I add that what the people intended by the Constitution is to be gathered solely from its text ; and that what the people intended by it and not what its framers or the commentators upon it intended, is the Constitution. So we will take up the text of the Constitution to learn what and what alone is the Constitution. Its very Preamble tells us that it is made to " secure the blessings of liberty." Thus, even in the porch of her temple doth Liberty deign to meet us. Strange, indeed, would it be were she to desert us in its apartments ! She does not. In our progress through the Constitution we find it pledging the power of the whole nation to maintain in every State " a republican form of government." Pro-slavery men tell us that this was no more than a republican government of the aristocratic Greek and Roman type; and that, therefore, men can consistently be bought and sold under it. But when the fathers gave us the Constitution, the political heavens were all ablaze with a new light—the light of the truth " that all men are created equal," and that the great end of government is to maintain that equality. Ere we get through the Constitution—ere Liberty has led us all the way through her temple—we meet with the slavery-forbidding declaration that: "No person shall be deprived of life, liberty, or property without due process of law."

I do not overlook the fact that the literal Constitution also is claimed to be on the side of slavery. The last clause which I quoted from it is claimed to be at least negatively so—for it is claimed to apply to the general Government only. But it is not the literal Constitution which says the application is to be restricted to the general Government. It is only this historical Constitution which says it. And, by the way, the history of the Constitution says the opposite also. The failure of Mr. Partridge's motion shows that it was not meant to have all the amendments apply to the general Government only; and that it was meant that the State governments should be restrained by some of them. The apportionment clause is held to recognize slavery. But it does not. Who then are the "three fifths of all other persons" it speaks of? They are aliens. Why do I say so? Because, using the word "free" in this clause in the sense authorized for ages by English law and usage, these three fifths are persons other than native and naturalized citizens — that is, aliens. (The argument of Lysander Spooner at this point in his admirable volume on the *Unconstitutionality of Slavery* is especially valuable.) Moreover, I say that they are aliens—because in this wise the clause is relieved of guilt. So, too, the migration and importation clause is held to recognize slavery. But it does not. Nothing is in the way of applying it to passengers and travelers. Whereas to apply it to slaves is to make it guilty of tolerating the slave-trade. And the clause respecting fugitives, who are "held to service or labor," is claimed to refer to slaves. But it should be applied to apprentices and hired laborers because, in its terms, it is entirely applicable to them. To apply it to slaves is to violate the accepted meaning of words. It is to go out of the way to make the Constitution infamous.

Let me here say, that, strictly speaking, I was wrong in taking the ground I did for vindicating my interpretation of the clauses just referred to. That ground was to save them from a guilty interpretation. But in legal contemplation they are incapable of a guilty interpretation. For, if there be in them the injustice generally attributed to them, nevertheless, as it is not clearly expressed, it is, legally speaking, unexpressed and unexisting. And how entirely reasonable is this legal view! For, is it not probable—to say the least, it is not certain, (and unless certain it is of no account,) that the people would have adopted the Constitution, had it said in plain terms that men should be rewarded for being slaveholders by a large addition to their political power and to their representation in the national councils; and that the horrid African slave-trade should continue for at least twenty years; and that our country should be sunk into a hunting-ground for human prey. Now it may be, as it is claimed it was, that it was attempted to get all this into the Constitution. But if the phraseologies were such that an honest, unsuspecting people would not see the guilty intention concealed in them, then what was intended became no part of the Constitution. All I have here said, and though, too, it had been far more strongly said, is justified by the rule which the Supreme Court of the United States laid down in the case against Fisher and others, 2d Cranch, 390 : " Where rights are infringed, where fundamental principles are overthrown, where the general system of the laws is departed from, the legislative intention must be expressed with *irresistible clearness* to induce a court of justice to suppose a design to effect such objects." I add, (what is obvious in the light of what has just been said,) that if the innocent interpretation, which I have given to the clauses in question, is not tenable, nevertheless in no event are the clauses susceptible of guilty interpretations.

Certain is it, then, that they who adopted the literal Constitution, did not adopt a pro-slavery one. Its words show they did not : and the fact that they had just then emerged from a bloody contest for human rights argues strongly that they would not. Whence then came our pro-slavery Constitution—our only recognized or actual Constitution during the last seventy years? It came from the cunning and wicked substitution by pro-slavery politicians of a pro-slavery historical Constitution for the anti-slavery literal one. For us, then, to agree upon an anti-slavery amendment of such terms, as would imply its necessity from the intrinsic character of the literal Constitution rather than from the pro-slavery character which we and our predecessors have foisted upon it ; for us thus to confound the anti-slavery literal Constitution with the pro-slavery historical one, which, in no small part through our own agency, has overridden it ; for us to confound the innocence of those who adopted the literal Constitution with our guilt in supplanting it with a pro-slavery one—would be a piece of wickedness and meanness from which may God save us ! May we be manly enough to consent to bear the burden of our own shame, instead of rolling it back upon our innocent ancestors !

Let me not be understood as finding fault with those brave sentinels of freedom, those faithful defenders of human rights—who, for twenty years, have been denouncing the Constitution. For it was only the pro-slavery historical Constitution, which they denounced. It was that, and that only, which they called a " covenant with death and agreement with hell ; " and richly did it deserve to be so called. It was only that one, which Mr. Garrison publicly burned ; and I admit that the fire of hell itself is not too hot for it to be cast into. True, it is that, on the occasion I refer to, he burnt the literal Constitution. Nevertheless in burning it he burnt not that, but only the pro-slavery interpretations of it—only its guilty misrepresentations. It was only these that he delivered " unto Satan." The Constitution was " saved."

I referred to our duty to the memory of the honest masses, whose votes gave us the Constitution. Nor should we forget our duty to those who will come after us. If we are so debauched by slavery as not to blush over our admission that the organic law of our nation is on the side of slavery, nevertheless, that our descendants will hang their heads over it, should restrain us from making it. If we, so far as our own sensibilities are concerned, can consent to have it go over the earth and down the ages that our fathers, in laying the foundations of our national existence, were moved by a spirit as wicked as that of the Thugs; and that "in order to form a more perfect union," they resolved to cement it with the blood of the slave; nevertheless let us remember that to our successors such a tradition will be a heritage of shame and sorrow. For slavery, having then passed away, they will not be corrupted by it, nor blinded to its character. It will in their eyes be the blackest of all crimes—blacker than even murder: and they will rather that the Constitution had been charged with sanctioning any other.

Dropping the figure of a historical Constitution, I am free to admit that the literal Constitution has been so long and so generally misrepresented and perverted, especially by pro-slavery courts and pro-slavery legislatures, that an amendment is desirable. As to whether it shall be made during the war or after the war, I would not be strenuous, nor add to what I have said on that point. Only let the amendment be in words that violate neither truth nor a sacred regard for the memory of the plain and honest men whose votes gave us the Constitution, and I will be content. It would be no more than is due to their memory; and no more than would be eagerly rendered to outraged justice and freedom, had it been white instead of black men who are the victims of the misinterpretation of the Constitution in regard to slavery—should the amendment admit in plain terms that it is a misinterpretation. But if this admission can not be obtained, is it too much to ask that the Amendment be a declaration, that the Constitution shall never be so interpreted as to legalize or permit the legalization of slavery, but shall ever be so interpreted as to prohibit slavery in every part of the nation? The usual words regarding involuntary servitude could be added. What an argument it is in favor of the anti-slavery character of the Constitution, that not so much as one line, no, nor one word of it, need be changed in order to bring it into perfect harmony with the most radical and sweeping anti-slavery Amendment! And how strongly is this character argued from the fact that were constitutional phrases, as innocent and inapplicable as these which are relied on to rob the noblest black man of his liberty, to be made the ground for robbing the meanest white man of his, or even the meanest white man of his meanest dog, such use of them would be instantly and indignantly scouted by all! And how strongly is it also argued from the fact, that a stranger to America and to her practice of making Church and State and all things minister to slavery, could see absolutely nothing, could suspect absolutely nothing in the Constitution, which might be seized on to turn that also to the foul and diabolical service!

But why should we stop with an anti-slavery amendment? Immeasurably more needed is an amendment to the effect that race or origin shall not work a forfeiture of any civil or political rights. Even an anti-slavery amendment may not be permanent. A race, whilst deprived of rights, which other races enjoy, can have no reasonable assurance that it will be protected against even slavery. But make it equal with them in rights, and it will be able to protect itself. It is said that to pour out upon the ballot-boxes the multitudinous and illiterate blacks of the slave States would be absurd. I do myself think so. I do myself think that in a State where a large share of the people can not read and write, reading and writing should be made conditions of voting.

I know not that the nation is prepared for such an amendment as I here suggest : and therefore I know not that it is prepared to escape destruction. God, in his awful controversy with us, demands entire justice for the race we have trampled on : and he will not be appeased by partial justice. Pharaoh, under the pressure of God's judgments, made concessions from time to time to the Israelites. Nevertheless he perished ; and left a memory, which still lives to warn both nations and individuals not to trust in a temporizing policy and in partial responses to justice.

And why, when Congress is submitting amendments, should it not submit one in favor of purging the Constitution of the aristocratic and people-distrusting Electoral Colleges, and of supplying their place with the right of the people to cast direct votes for President and Vice-President? And why not one against polygamy? And how beautifully seasonable it would be, if, now when we are suffering because we denied God's authority in national concerns, and blasphemously held slave-law to be paramount to the "higher law," we should penitently and adoringly insert between "do" and "ordain" in the Preamble of the Constitution : "whilst recognizing the supreme authority of God over nations as well as individuals!"

But it is objected that the anti-slavery amendment would be an encroachment on "State sovereignty," and the like objection would doubtless be made to these other amendments. Nevertheless, this proud "State sovereignty" can not help itself. Its exposure to be reduced to a very humble minimum of power will last as long as the right to amend the Constitution shall last.

By the way, this right of amendment is the most valuable of all our constitutional rights. Without it, a State might set up and keep up systems that would pour their corrupting and destroying influences over the whole nation. With it, the intellectually and morally advanced States, if they number three fourths of all, are able to drag up to their own higher plane of civilization the other and lagging fourth. In the progress of knowledge and truth and justice three fourths of the States may ere long be ashamed of a

nation in which woman is treated as an inferior, and political
power withheld from her: and so, too, they may ere long be
ashamed of a nation in which Government, whose sole legitimate
province is to protect person and property, does more than all
else to endanger person and property by permitting and authorizing the alcoholic manufacture of maniacs: and ere long they
may also be ashamed of a nation, which, setting no limits to
individual acquisition of land, allows millions to be landless,
whose right to the soil is as natural, perfect, and sacred as the
right to light or air.   I say *ere long*—for in our present school of
suffering we shall be like to grow fast both in the knowledge and
acknowledgment of human rights. Nothing, so much as affliction,
is promotive of wisdom and goodness.   "The Captain of salvation was made perfect through suffering."   But whether it be
sooner or later that as many as three fourths of the States shall
desire the reformation of the nation in these respects, happy,
thrice happy, will it be that, by means of their power to amend
the Constitution, this desire can be gratified.   I do not forget
that this power can be wielded for a retrograde as well as for a
forward movement.   But our nation is suffering so much for her
sins, and especially for her sin of placing the Constitution on the
side of wickedness; and she is, moreover, learning so much from
her sufferings, that I have little fear she will ever again be disposed to place it on that side.   She placed it there by misinter-
preting it on the question of slavery; and sorely has she suffered
from doing so.   She will not consent to amendments of the Constitution, which will again make it the servant of wickedness.

THE CONSTITUTION, RECONSTRUCTION, AND THE PROCLAMATION.

SPEECH AT COOPER INSTITUTE, NEW-YORK.

January 4, 1865.

————•••————

It is proposed to have the Constitution so amended that henceforth slavery shall not be law in any part of the land. But has it ever been ? If so, what made it law ? By not being forbidden in the Constitution, is one answer to the question. But it is forbidden in it—directly as well as indirectly, by its letter as well as by its spirit, by itself as well as by its preamble.

It is held that the States made the Constitution. If they did, they nevertheless made it, as the preamble shows, in the name of the people. Moreover, as they made it in the name not of this nor that sort of people; and made it "to secure the blessings of liberty " not to this nor that sort of people, so it is to be interpreted as having been made in the name of the whole people and for the whole people, and as forbidding the enslavement of any portion or any variety of the people. That this doctrine that the States made the Constitution has obtained so long and so widely, is not strange. There are thousands of doctrines, and this is one of them, which are upheld not by their soundness, for they are utterly unsound, but by the interest which men have to uphold them. There is but one fact of any moment which favors this doctrine that the States made the Constitution: and even this but seems to favor it. The fact I refer to is, that the people voted by States upon the Constitution. They did so, in the first place, for the sake of convenience. But in the second place, from necessity—the people of each State having to say for themselves and by themselves whether they would consent to such a modifying and curtailing of the rights and powers of their State as the erection of the proposed Government called for. Clearly, the people of Virginia and the people of New-York could not act either for each other or together in this matter.

But to return to my declaration that slavery is forbidden in the Constitution. I will mention a few of the instances in which it is forbidden. The right of the people, without any exception, to keep and bear arms, and the right of Congress to make contracts with whom it will without exception, to serve in the army and

62

GERRIT SMITH ON THE REBELLION.

navy, are rights which imply that all the people are free. The re-
quirement of "a republican form of government" in every State
is a virtual prohibition of slavery. For we must bear in mind
that our fathers did not mean by "republican form of government" one of the Greek or Roman aristocratic type. They had
just said in the Declaration of Independence "that all men are
created equal." Their choice of a government, therefore, would
be one to defend this equality—would be one whose subjects
would be equal before the law. But the strongest and most
direct prohibition of slavery in the Constitution is its declaration
that, "No person shall be deprived of life, liberty, or property
without due process of law"—that is, without a trial and conviction according to the course of the common law.

It is, however, said that, inasmuch as there are clauses in the Constitution which permit slavery, those in it which appear to forbid it
are not to be construed as forbidding it. But which are those that
permit it? The answer is, the apportionment clause, and the migration and importation clause, and the fugitive-servant clause.
Certainly, not on their face do they permit it. You must go outside of the text of the Constitution for help to give them this construction; and that you have no right to do. To give an innocent
construction to the uncertain words of a law you may go outside
of the law. But where a guilty construction is your aim, you are
shut up to the text: and the text fails you, unless it is with "irresistible clearness" on the side of the guilty construction. Says
the Supreme Court of the United States, 2 Cranch, 390: "Where
rights are infringed, where fundamental principles are overthrown, where the general system of the laws is departed from,
the legislative intention must be expressed with irresistible clearness to induce a court of justice to suppose a design to effect such
objects."

I may be asked, to whom, then, do these clauses refer, if they
do not refer to slaves? I am not bound to answer. I will, however, say that, without the least violence to its language, the apportionment clause might be applied to aliens, aliens being destitute of those rights and privileges the possessors of which the
English law had for so many ages called "free." And I would
say that the language of the importation and migration clause
permits its application to travelers and passengers. And, also,
that the fugitive-servant clause does, under its simplest construction, apply to apprentices and hired laborers. But whether these
clauses are or are not capable of these applications, it is enough
for our present purpose that the canon of legal interpretation
forbids their application to slaves.

It is said that the framers of the Constitution intended to put
it on the side of slavery. Probably some of them did. For there
is historical evidence, as well that some of them were pro-slavery
as that others were anti-slavery. But may we not argue that the
pro-slavery spirit was repented of when we see that, four days
before they closed their Convention, the framers unanimously .

struck out "servitude" from the Constitution and supplied its
place with "service," for the avowed reason that "servitude"
expresses the condition of slaves, and "service" that of freemen?
What, however, the framers intended the Constitution to be, is
of little more consequence than what the scrivener who writes it
intends by the deed of the land. What the grantor and grantee
intend, is the question in the one case; and what the adopters of the
Constitution intended, is the question in the other. What the
adopters intended, is to be gathered solely from its text. For it was
not the discussions nor intentions of the framers, nor the histories
of the making and objects of the Constitution which were adopted.
It was the text only: and, as we have seen, the text admits of no
guilty construction, because it expresses no guilty intention. I
add that if the framers intended to put the Constitution on the
side of slavery, they should, in terms of "irresistible clearness,"
have apprised the people of the guilty intention. Did they wish
the people to encourage and reward slaveholding by a special and
large representation in our national councils? Did they wish
them to sanction the abominations of the slave-trade? Did they
wish them to convert the whole nation into a hunting-ground for
human prey?—then they should have asked for all this in plain
terms and in words of unmistakable meaning. Had they, however, done so, the people would have scouted the insolence. But
in no other terms and words could they ask the people to make
themselves guilty of such stupendous wickedness—the laws of
legal interpretation making it impossible to ask it in other terms
and words.

How immeasurably absurd it is to call the Constitution pro-
slavery is seen in the fact, that it needs not the slightest alteration
in line or letter to be entirely harmonious with the most thorough
anti-slavery amendment; and in the further fact, that a stranger
to the history of America would not so much as suspect that there
is slavery in her Constitution; and in the still further fact, that
to apply to the enslavement of a white man clauses which no
more point and express themselves to this end than do the clauses
in question to the end of enslaving the black man, would be held
by all to be ridiculous, insulting, and infamous to the last degree.

But although slavery is repeatedly forbidden in the Constitution, and nowhere in it permitted, nevertheless I would not only not
oppose but I would favor such an amendment of it as would in
plain and literal terms forbid slavery. A sufficient reason for
such an amendment is, that the Constitution has been so contin-
uously and thoroughly perverted to the upholding of slavery.
War, however, with all its excitements and distractions, is not the
best time for altering the organic law of a nation. That solemn
work needs all the leisure, calmness, and composure which peace
brings. Then, too, we need to be absorbed in the one purpose—
and one work of succeeding in the war. Is it said that slavery is
in the way of such success? I answer that we need not amend
the Constitution in order to put it out of the way. That can be

done quicker than by amending the Constitution. Nevertheless, I would waive all question in regard to the time for amending the Constitution, and be concerned only about the terms of the amendment. To have it in such terms as would imply that without it the Constitution is for slavery, would be to wrong and blot the memory of the honest, unsuspecting masses who adopted the Constitution ; to disgrace our nation in the eyes of other nations ; and to make our posterity ashamed of both ancestry and nation. If the amendment shall not be such, as to say in plain terms that the Constitution is against slavery, it should at least be such as to imply it. If the amendment shall not go so far as to say that the interpretation of the Constitution for slavery is a misinterpretation, nevertheless it should at least imply that it is ; and this it would imply if it should declare that the Constitution shall never be so interpreted as to legalize or permit the legalization of slavery, but shall ever be so interpreted as to forbid both.

I said that slavery can be put out of the way quicker than by amending the Constitution. The constitutional right of Congress to declare war carries with it the constitutional right to conduct war. Moreover, the Constitution expressly empowers Congress "to make all laws which shall be necessary and proper" to this end. Congress alone is to decide upon the necessity and propriety. If in its judgment the successful prosecution of the war calls for the abolition of slavery, then it is to abolish it ; if for the abolition of apprenticeship, then it is to abolish apprenticeship also. I go further, and say that, if, in time of war, the preaching and teaching in all the churches and school-houses become disloyal, it may shut up all the churches and school-houses. A democratic people are wont to be jealous of absolute power; and this may account for the injurious hesitation of Congress during this war to assert such power, notwithstanding it is, in respect to war, so clearly clothed with it. For a nation to disclaim absolute power for carrying on war is to acknowledge her incompetence to carry on war, and to apprise her sister nations that whichever of them is looking for an easy prey can look toward her.

I said that Congress has the constitutional right to conduct war. But, as I shall say more fully hereafter, such a war as that we are now involved in is to be conducted, not according to the Constitution, but according to the law of war.

To return to my subject—we are under a strong temptation to hold that the Constitution is for slavery. For if it is, then the fathers, who gave it to us, must, of course, share very largely in the guilt of ten to twenty millions being born in slavery, and in the guilt of this rebellion, which has come of slavery, and which is soaking our land with our best blood. But if it is not in itself on the side of slavery, then they, including ourselves, who have put it there, are the party responsible for these seventy-six years of slavery, for all its wickedness and all its woes. We have seen, however, that the Constitution is not for slavery. And now will we, in order to lighten the shame and reduce the criminality of our pro-slavery practice under it, declare that the Constitution is for slavery? This is the question. Let us answer it in a way honorable to the fathers, and honorable, also, to our penitent selves, by so framing the amendment that it shall take the blame from them and put it on their successors. I do not like to say that this would be magnanimity. It would be but simple justice.

Let me here say, that there is another amendment to the Constitution, which is more needed than one against slavery. It is one which shall save men from losing civil or political rights because of their race or origin. Such an amendment would not only banish slavery, but it would afford an effectual protection against its return. Accord to men the full measure of their civil and political rights, and they can defend themselves against slavery. Their freedom will then stand not in the uncertain will and shifting policy of others; but where alone it should stand, in their own strength. This nation wants peace with man. But more does it need peace with God. And yet how can it ever have peace with God so long as it continues to quarrel with Him for having divided the human family into races, and to punish Him for the division by denying to some of these races the rights of manhood!

By the way, this power to amend the Constitution is its most important power. By means of it we can put an end to slavery in one State and to polygamy in another, and to other abominations in other States. In a word, we can, by means of it, make all the States alike in respect to their chief systems and policies, and, therefore, all the people homogeneous and so far happy.

I will, in this connection, say something on the Reconstruction of the Rebel States. Throughout the war I have regarded any Reconstruction of them before the war shall be ended as premature. In other words, I have held that the provisional governments, which we set up in the wake of our conquering armies, should not be supplanted with permanent ones until the rebellion is subdued. I have held this, because, in the first place, we should be too much occupied with the war to be building permanent governments; and because, in the second place, of my fear—a fear justified by the present—that Reconstruction, if it should precede the complete crushing of the rebellion, would have in it as fatally unsound materials as had the image seen by Nebuchadnezzar. But as the policy of a *present* Reconstruction has prevailed, all we can do is to contribute to give the right shape to the Reconstruction.

And here let me say, that the same state of mind which has led me to oppose Reconstruction, has led me to oppose all negotiations for peace. Fatally derogatory is it to our national dignity, utterly at war is it with every just consideration, to treat with armed rebels, and especially such rebels. They took up arms without cause. Therefore, they must lay them down without conditions.

The plan of Reconstruction before Congress has many excellent features. Particularly welcome are its provisions against allowing

disloyalists of the higher civil and military ranks to vote for
members of the legislature or for governor, and against allowing slavery to exist, and against allowing the Reconstructed
States to be charged with any part of the rebel debt. But
deeply do I regret that a provision, more important than any
or all of these, should have been omitted. I mean a provision
against allowing race or origin to work a forfeiture of civil or
political rights. This omission may prove as fatal to the standing of the Reconstruction as did the clay in its feet to the
standing of Nebuchadnezzar's image.

But it is said that suffrage is a matter for State regulation. I
admit it, as a general proposition. I admit that, but for the war,
no one would have thought of taking the regulation of it out of
the hands of the State. But the war has made national action at
this point not only proper, but imperative. The question now is,
not what would have been due to the rebel States had they not rebelled, but what restrictions is it necessary to put upon them, now
that they have rebelled? The question now is, not what would
have been due to them had they remained our friends, but what
securities shall we provide, now that they have become our foes?
In a word, the question now is, what concessions the conqueror
can wisely and safely make to the conquered? I say the conqueror, for Reconstruction assumes that we are sure and soon to
be the conqueror.

Then, again, this plan of Reconstruction provides that certain
persons shall not be allowed to vote. And is not this as great
and as humiliating a restriction upon State powers, as would be a
provision that certain persons shall be allowed to vote?

All through this war the delusion has obtained extensively, that
the States which flung away the Constitution have still their
former rights under it. But they lost them all when they rebelled.

The word "white" being in the plan, the blacks will, of course,
be shut out from all part in making the organic law of a Reconstructed State. But even were this word not in, nevertheless, as
the plan does not require suffrage for the blacks, there is not the
least probability that they would get it. Numerous, and conclusive as numerous, are the reasons why the plan should require it.

1st. Though before the war we had not the right to demand
suffrage for them, we have it now. We have paid for the right
in much treasure and blood.

2d. We owe them suffrage because it is vital to them to have
it; because, without it, they will be exposed to every wrong and
every oppression : and we owe it to them because they are our
saviours. But for their sympathy with our cause, our nation
would have perished.

3d. We owe them suffrage for the sake of the South. It is
her contempt of human rights that has barbarized her—that
has demonized her. For demons must they have become, who
can treat prisoners of war as they treat them. She must be

recovered from her barbarism and demonism, and contempt of man ; and this cannot be done so long as the ballot is withheld from her blacks.

4th. We must secure suffrage to them, in order to save the loyal whites of the South. Black voters can be the only effectual breakwater against the fury of disloyal Southrons toward loyal Southrons.

5th. For the nation's sake, we must insist on suffrage for the blacks. To leave the political power of the South exclusively in the hands of her whites, would be to leave her to repeat her crimes and savagery, not only upon her blacks, but upon the nation.

6th. The whole world will loathe and abhor us, if now, when the negroes have saved us, we shall leave them helpless in the hands of their enemies—enemies, too, who, because they have saved us, will hate them more than ever.

7th. God's controversy with us will still remain, if we shall still persist in refusing rights to those whom He has chosen to wrap in black skins. Can we afford the continuance of a controversy, which has already cost us so much treasure and blood ?

But it is said that we are inconsistent in requiring the Government to exact suffrage for the Southern blacks, whilst the Northern blacks are generally deprived of it. No, we are not. Though such deprivation is unreasonable and wicked, the Government has not the power to forbid it. Moreover, lack of suffrage does not expose Northern blacks to such wrongs as it does Southern blacks ; nor does it so peril our nation in the one case as it does in the other.

It is also said that we are inconsistent in making so much account of having the Southern black men vote, whilst the Northern women are denied suffrage. I admit the utter injustice of this denial. But it must be remembered that they who vote for women are their friends—their husbands, fathers, brothers, sons ; whilst they who vote for the Southern blacks are their despisers and haters. So, too, it must be remembered that the denial of suffrage in the one case is not fraught with the peril that it is in the other.

I may be asked whether I would have entirely illiterate persons allowed to vote. I answer, that where they are but a small portion of the people, I would ; but that, where they are a large one, I would not, unless there be some special reason demanding it. If the disloyal whites of the South shall be denied a vote, (and even the humblest of them should in this respect be put upon a probation of at least a dozen years,) then let it be required of the blacks, in common with the whites, that they shall be able to read and write before being allowed to vote. But if the disloyal whites of the South shall be allowed to vote forthwith, then, by all that is reasonable and righteous, by all that we owe to the loyal blacks, and by all that our national safety calls for, those loyal blacks should also be allowed to vote forthwith. Surely, surely, this is but a very moderate claim.

I own it is bad to have ignorance vote. But infinitely worse is it to have disloyalty vote. Welcome, loyal ignorance: but no patience with disloyal intelligence.

Many say that the abolition of slavery should content us for the present, and that we should wait patiently for further instalments of justice to the black man. But if now, under all the force and freshness of his claims upon our gratitude, we can be so base as to withhold any of his essential rights, very little has he to hope from us in the future.

It is but too plain that if the Reconstruction Bill now before Congress shall become a law, the blacks of the rebel States will be denied suffrage, and their whites alone will have it; the loyal element in their population will be denied it, and the disloyal element will have it; in still other words, our friends in those States will have no political power, and our enemies in them have all. Not to speak of the deep injustice and cruel ingratitude of thus treating those who have saved us, what folly, what madness is it, to trifle in this wise with the future of our nation! Horrid as is the present war, it has not sufficed to bring the nation to repentance. A more horrid one may be necessary. Were I not an abolitionist, I would, if this Bill succeed, predict a war of races at the South. But I remember that abolition prophets are treated as Cassandras—as unworthy of the least belief. For twenty years they were foretelling (even on the floor of Congress it was foretold) that slavery, unless put away peaceably, would soon and surely go out in blood. But their predictions were only laughed at.

Louisiana, considering the circumstances, made a very creditable approach to justice. Her Constitution, far better at this point than that of our own State, permits her Legislature to make voters of her black men: and in such circumstances a permission falls little short of a command. Had the plan before Congress prohibited the forfeiture of civil or political rights, by reason of race or origin, I should, notwithstanding her Constitution falls short of such prohibition, have been reluctant to oppose the reëntrance of Louisiana into the sisterhood of States. The other Reconstructed States, being right at this vital point, she would soon have been also. But they being wrong, she will be far more likely to sink to their level than to lift up her advanced Constitution into the full recognition of the equal rights of all men.

Speaking of Louisiana, brings to my mind the censures cast by some of the radical abolitionists upon General Banks. I trust that these censures are entirely undeserved. I regard him not only as a brave, patriotic, and able man, but as a sincere friend of the colored race. I thanked and loved him, when I read of his having the little black girl lifted up on the cannon. He might not have meant by it all that it symbolized. But, to me, it was the lifting up of the representative of her race from feebleness to strength.

To me, this child's riding on the cannon foreshadowed the triumphant progress of that race. And I am informed that the liberal feature in the Constitution of Louisiana, to which I have referred, is due preëminently to General Banks.

Her Constitution puts an end to slavery in Louisiana. There are some restraints, notwithstanding, upon those who were so recently its victims. I trust that they are no more and no greater than the perils and exigencies of war call for; and that they will all be withdrawn upon the return of peace. I confess, however, that there is no certainty that justice, at any point, will be done to the black man in any rebel or, indeed, in any anti-rebel State in which the right of suffrage is denied him.

But, to return from this digression, I trust I made it plain that the Constitution does in various clauses forbid slavery. Plain, too, I might have made it, that in its whole spirit and tenor it forbids it. But what if it did not, would therefore, be law? Must piracy and murder be forbidden by the Constitution in order that they be not law? Much less need slavery, a worse crime than either, be forbidden by it in order that it be not law. I trust, too, that I made it plain that those clauses of the Constitution, which are relied on to prove that it permits slavery, do not permit it. Let me now add that even if the Constitution did permit slavery, slavery would not be law. All will admit that no words, however strong or ingeniously chosen and arranged, could suffice to make piracy law. How emphatic, then, must be the incapacity of slavery to be law! For, amongst all the piracies of earth, slavery is the superlative piracy. Indeed, what other piracy is not reduced to a mere peccadillo, when brought into comparison with the overshadowing slaveholding piracy! So, too, all will admit that no words can make murder law. But the crime of murder, like that of piracy, is outdone by the crime of slavery. Every wise parent had far rather his child were murdered than enslaved. The murdered is killed but once. The slave is "killed all the day long." The murdered is robbed but of life. The slave, robbed of all except life, is cursed with remaining life instead of being relieved by death. Murder kills but the body. Slavery the soul. Murder does not degrade the manhood of the murdered. Slavery makes merchandise of manhood. Murder denies not that its victim was placed by God upon the heights of immortality. But slavery drags down its victim from those glorious heights to the category of brutes and things. Murder kills but a few, and spares the masses to unfold their powers and reach after every enjoyment. But slavery allows a few to tyrannize over the masses, and worse than murder them by working and whipping them worse than brutes are worked and whipped; by robbing them of their right to letters and wages and marriage; and by leaving them no rights whatever whereby to protect themselves from the storm of wrongs and outrages which sweeps incessantly over their lot.

I have argued that nothing can make slavery law. I go farther,

and say that law can not be made. And here I have reached a
point where more than at any other, the world needs to be rev-
olutionized. This making of law, of civil, theological, and other
law, has made up the greater part of human sorrows. Law-mak-
ers there never should have been—only law-declarers : and these
should have declared nothing to be law but what is natural. Nature alone is our law, and only so far as we let her, and her alone,
be law unto us, do we or can we honor the God of nature. An
enactment that wood is iron or iron wood would be void, because
at war with nature. For the same reason an enactment to en-
slave a man, that is to transmute him into a chattel, is void. The
legislature is to leave wood to be wood, iron to be iron, and man
to be man. Advancing wisdom and civilization will yet bring
the courts to this ground. They will yet hold that whatever
tramples upon or ignores nature is not law. I do not mean they
will hold that to be no law, which simply goes beyond or falls
short of the demands of nature. For instance, interest or the
use of money is reasonable, and, therefore, agreeable to nature.
The legislature, in regulating the rates, may go too high or too
low. Nevertheless, as the subject-matter does not confront nature, the courts will not confront the legislature. So, too, where
the legislature is regulating the punishment due to crimes, the subject-matter is one not in conflict but in harmony with nature ; and,
therefore, though in one instance the prescribed punishment may
be excessive and in another deficient, the courts, nevertheless, will
feel themselves bound by the will of the legislature. But where,
as in the case of enslaving or chattelizing men, the subject-matter
is itself foreign to nature and an outrage upon nature, there the
courts will hold that there is no law to interpret, and that the
action of the legislature is void. In other words, where the subject-matter of the legislation sets aside nature, the courts will set
aside the legislation.

Will the Supreme Court of the United States ever rise up to
this level of reason and nature ? Will this Court, hitherto guilty
of so much unreasonableness and unnaturalness, at last yield itself
to these high claims of reason and nature ? Will this Court, so
long a bulwark of slavery, become a bulwark of freedom ? It
will when it shall pronounce the truth that slavery, containing in
itself nothing of right, nor reason, nor nature, is therefore destitute
of all the elements of law, and is no law : and that, containing in
itself the grossest and guiltiest violations of right, and reason,
and nature, it is to be pursued as the most execrable outlaw. So
preëminently instructive have been the lessons of the last few
years, that possibly several members of this Court are already
educated up to the necessary preparation for pronouncing this
conclusive truth against all the pretensions of slavery. There is a
man in this land—he is emphatically a man—whom I have long
known, and as long admired and loved. He was once in a very
small minority, and as poor in the public favor as were we, who
were his fellow-laborers, and were identified with him in both

cause and party. But so swift of late years has been the wheel
of revolution in this country, that he is now one of the members
of that Court. I trust that I shall not be regarded as violating
the sacredness of private correspondence, when I say that as long
as nine years ago this noble man, in speaking of slavery, declared:
" I shall rejoice to witness such progress in society, that courts
will regard the total denial of rights as so contrary to the law of
nature, that no legislative enactment can entitle it to recognition."
And again, a few weeks after: "With you, I am for freedom
everywhere and for slavery nowhere; for freedom for all, and
slavery for none. Most heartily will I rejoice when the people
and their judges shall be educated up to the point of regarding
slavery as so great a wrong that it can not be legalized." Mark
his words: "and their judges"! And now, behold, he is himself
one of their judges! ay, and their chief judge ! Then, eight years
ago, he said: "If you can find me judges, who will decide that slavery
is so clearly and palpably repugnant to reason and natural justice,
that it can be sustained nowhere and by no law, I shall be the
last man to object to the decision." Again, mark his words: "If
you can find me judges"! And lo, he finds himself one of their
judges! ay, and at such a time as this! a time when Providence
has so wondrously prepared the way for the Supreme Court of
the United States to render signal service to humanity. Well
might we apostrophize our new Chief Justice in the words of
Mordecai to Esther: "And who knoweth whether thou art come
to the kingdom for such a time as this ?"

I am sure that my friend will pardon me for the liberty I have
taken with his letters. It honors him to make public the wise
words I have quoted from them. That it does mankind good,
will, however, go farther to gain me his forgiveness. Precious
words were these to me when I received them! Precious words
to one who, through many years of reproach and discouragement,
had been invoking such utterances from leading minds!

Let me here say that, in adverting to those great duties with
which great passing events are charging the Supreme Court, I
had no reference to the Proclamations of Freedom. I assume
that this Court will recognize the validity of those papers and
rejoice in their operation. An insurrection, involving but a County,
or even one involving a whole State, may very properly be met
by Constitutional law only—by that law of which that Court is
the interpreter. But the war which many millions are waging
against us—so many that the nations, including even our own,
have been constrained to accord belligerent rights to them—
is one not to be conducted by the provisions of the Constitution. A war of such magnitude is to be conducted in accordance with International Law. I confess that I see no reason why the President's military acts in this war, any more
than Grant's or Farragut's, should be questioned by the Supreme
Court. These Proclamations and their Orders are alike amenable
to the law of war, and to that law only. Both the Proclamations

and the Orders may often come incidentally before this Court: but so long as it sees them to be in accordance with the law of war, it will not stand in their way.

Just here I might be asked whether I hold that such of the slaves within the scope of the President's Proclamation of first January, 1863, as shall be still in the hands of the enemy at the close of the war, will be entitled to freedom by virtue of that Proclamation. My answer would be that I do. I go farther, and say that the war should never be closed, nay, can never be closed, until they are free.

And now some of you are ready to quote Vattel and Grotius, and other publicists, to prove that the property of our enemy in war is not ours until we have reduced it to actual possession. My reply is, that slaves are not property, but men; and that in all our reasoning in the case we shall, provided we are ourselves men, treat them as men.

The Proclamation on its face set the slaves within its purview unconditionally free. Its friends hold that it did set them unconditionally free. I am amongst its friends. Nevertheless, I hold that it did not. It proffered them freedom on a condition—a condition none the less real because unexpressed. This condition was the proper response of the slaves to the Proclamation. Had they flouted it, refused its boon, and preferred working and fighting for our enemy, would any thing have been due them by virtue of the Proclamation? Certainly not. The Proclamation was made to win them to us; and they had no right to profit by it, if they refused to be won to us. So far as they have not fulfilled this implied condition in the Proclamation, we owe them nothing by reason of the Proclamation. So far as they have, we are their debtors.

And now the way is prepared to inquire what classes and portions of the slaves in question it would be right for us to leave in slavery.

First. Shall the wives and children of those who have escaped to us, and have fought for us, be left in slavery? Shall the wives and children of those who have recently come to us, and of those who shall come to us, be left in slavery? Shall, for instance, the mothers, wives and children, who begged and wept to be allowed to come along with Sherman's army, and with their sons, husbands and fathers, who had joined it, be left in slavery? To all these questions you will return an emphatic "No."

Second. Shall the families of the slaves, who were detected in their attempt to get within our lines, and were flogged to death, or otherwise put to death, be left in slavery? Or shall they who survived their punishment for such offense, or shall their families, be left in slavery? Here again you are quick to say, "No."

Third. Shall the slaves too aged and infirm to do more than advise and encourage the young and strong to peril all to get to us and help us, and too poor to do more than make up for each that little bundle of rags that is the sum total of the worldly goods with which the slave sets out in his adventure, and who with their whole heart do all this—shall they be left in slavery? Not with your consent.

Fourth. Shall those old slave saints, to whose glowing prayers in behalf of our cause God loves to listen, and whose bodily feebleness disables them from doing more for us than pray—shall they be left in slavery? You protest against it.

Fifth. Shall any of these millions, whose hearts are with us, and who have done for us what they could, though they have not been able to get to us—shall they be left in slavery? By no means, is your answer.

Sixth. Shall any, who have suffered from the Proclamation by reason of being brought under a stricter surveillance, and of being made the objects of increased jealousy and hatred, and this especially because of their attempts, or discovered desires, to avail themselves of the Proclamation—shall any of these be left in slavery? Earnestly would you oppose it.

And now, after all these exceptions, what classes or portions of the slaves within the scope of the Proclamation would there be to be left in slavery? I know of none. If there be amongst all these slaves an individual, who out of his wicked heart chooses the side of the enemy, I admit that the Proclamation owes him nothing, though I do not admit that even he deserves to be a slave. No man is bad enough to deserve that.

I proceed to say that the implied contract in the Proclamation between the nation and the slaves, has been faithfully fulfilled on their part; that, under the invitations and promises of the Proclamation, they have done what they could for us; and that now it remains for the nation to fulfill on its part. For her not to do so would be to disgrace herself with the most signal instance of perfidy toward the helpless and worthy poor which the world has ever seen. Many fear that the President will shuffle off his responsibilities in this case upon the Supreme Court. I do not. He is an eminently wise and good man; and he can not fail to see that it is for him to fulfill, on the part of the nation, her contract with the slaves. He will not leave their freedom to any contingency. Have no fear that he will overshadow his well-earned fame with eternal infamy. A simple parallel, and I will pass on from the Proclamation to other topics. Suppose Sherman, believing it to be vital to his success to secure the friendship and help of a certain village or city in his way through Georgia, had proposed to stand by it if it would stand by him—to allow it to take hold of the strength of his army and his nation if it would consent to give up its hold upon the Confederacy. And then suppose that the proposition, having been accepted and faithfully lived up to by the village or city, Sherman should shirk his responsibilities and leave it to some one else to say what should be done on his part. The curses of the world would fall upon him so thick and so hot, as to wither up the last feather in the proud plumes of his military

glory. And now for the parallel. The President, who, like
Sherman, is also a military commander, and who acted in the
case solely as such—for he had no right to act in it in any other
capacity—the President, I say, seeing the straits to which our
nation was reduced, and that it was on the brink of ruin, proposed
to save it by obtaining the friendship and help of the slaves. To
this end he promised them, provided they would cast in their lot
with us, their freedom, and to maintain it by the whole power of the
nation, and to honor such as were "of suitable condition" with
places in "the armed service of the United States." Moreover,
he invoked "the considerate judgment of mankind and the gra-
cious favor of Almighty God" upon the promise.

Time has verified the wisdom of this great measure of the President. The measure has brought salvation to our country. God
forbid that we should throw away the salvation, as to no small
extent we shall, if the Reconstruction policy shall be such as to
leave a vestige of slavery, or even such as to leave the loyal element
of the Southern population politically disabled, and therefore an
easy prey to the disloyal element!

I said that the Proclamation had brought salvation to our
country. The slaves fulfilled on their part the implied contract
in the Proclamation, and thus became our saviours. Those of
them who could, came to us; and those who could not come to
us, nevertheless worked for us, as far as they could. Fear not
that the President will requite this devotion to our cause with the
leaving of a portion of these saviours in slavery. The bargain he
made with them he will not break. Better that the nation perish
than that such a bargain be broken !

But to return to the line of argument which I was pursuing
before I struck off upon the Proclamation. I had argued that
where the subject-matter of the legislation, such as the enslaving
or chattelizing of men, is at war with nature, there can be no law.
I now add that nothing is law which can not be administered in
the spirit of honesty. Every judge, every commissioner, who
remanded his poor trembling brother into slavery, knew that he
was dishonest in doing so—knew that he was not doing as he
would be done by. For he knew that, were he a slave, he would
not recognize slavery to be law, and therefore obligatory upon his
conscience. For he knew that, were he a slave, he would escape
if he could ; that he would mount his master's fleetest horse if he
could ; that he would shoot his pursuing master if he could.

This is indeed a horrid war through which we are passing.
We are working out, in treasure and tears and blood incomput-
able, the heavy penalty of our crimes against Freedom and Justice.
God pity the tens of thousands whom this war has maimed and
disabled for life ! God pity the ten thousand families whom it
has bereaved and desolated ! God pity the countless poor under
its crushing burdens ! And yet great good is to come of this
war. The greatest of all the good will be the higher appreciation
of man. This war is a judgment upon us for our disparagement

and contempt of man. Its terrible lessons are teaching us to disparage and contemn him no longer. Am I told that we did hold him in esteem? I answer that it was his accidents rather than his essence. For instance, he was esteemed who was white, or wealthy, or wise, polished or promoted. But he who had but mere manhood to commend him, was made little account of. Constitutions and creeds were held sacred and inviolable. But man, "the one sole sacred thing beneath the cope of heaven," alas, how cheap! Surely, no right-minded man can say of this war, "To what purpose is this waste?" even if he look no farther than to the fact that the highest judicial place, so recently occupied by one who could not associate the rights of manhood with a black skin, is now occupied by one who holds, not only that "a man's a man for a' that," but that, under whatever misfortune of calamities, nay, under whatever guilt of crimes, the rights of manhood remain indestructible.

I said that man will be more appreciated in consequence of this war. I add that this new appreciation will give us new and better laws and new and better judicial interpretations of them. Legislatures and courts sink or rise as the regard for man sinks or rises. The one legitimate end of law upon earth is the protection of human rights. Nevertheless, the earth over, man has been held in so low esteem, that, the earth over, legislatures and courts have done scarcely less for the destruction than for the protection of human rights. I said that law on earth is solely for the protection of human rights. Many add—and of divine rights also. I do not. I hold that God is wise and strong enough to take care of His own rights; and that He bids us take care of ours, and leave Him to take care of His. We best honor God's rights in upholding man's. Under this accursed plea of looking after God's rights, humanity has, in all ages, suffered its heaviest woes. From this has come the worst type of bigotry, intolerance, persecution. From this have come, not only the Inquisition, but numberless forms of torture for both the body and the soul. Even so intelligent a man as Alexander H. Stephens falls back for his justification of slavery on this fanatical regard for God's rights. For, like most others, he interprets the belchings of drunken Noah into a curse of God—a curse, it is true, on Canaan: but, by one of those frequent ecclesiastical accommodations, on poor Africa also.

But I must close. It is not better laws only that we need. We need a better religion also. Our laws have been on the side of oppression. Our religion has gone to the polls and voted for the buyers and sellers of men. How shall we get better laws and a better religion? Only by getting juster and higher conceptions of the dignity, and grandeur, and sacredness of man. Our laws and our religion will conform precisely to those conceptions. Contemptible will be the laws and religion of every people who think contemptuously of man. But beautiful and blessed will be the laws and the religion which reverence human nature, even when in its lowest condition—even when in ignorance, and rags, and chains. This is the religion which Jesus taught. He lived, and labored, and died, not for this nor that sort of men, but for all men; not for men of these or those characteristics, these or those surroundings, these or those accidents, but for men of whatever type, or condition, or character. He identified himself with all men, simply because they were men.

I am old, and shall not live to see it : and you, who are young, may not. But the day is coming—it is hastening on—when, all over this broad and beautiful land, nature, so dear to all who give themselves up to the study of her, so sure in her guidance, so full of instructions, so full of God, shall inspire and mould both laws and religion. Come, blessed day! Come quickly! And then the natural rights of men shall no more be invaded in the name of law, nor in the name of religion. Then Civil Government, no more their oppressor, will be the strength of the weak and the shield of the defenseless. Then the Church, no longer the betrayer of the poor, and no longer leaguing itself with and voting with the enemies of the poor, will be their peaceful haven from the storms that pelt them without ; their resting-place from persecutions ; their inviting bosom of pity and love.

www.ingramcontent.com/pod-product-compliance
Lightning Source LLC
Chambersburg PA
CBHW030557270326
41927CB00007B/965